A2

US Government and Politics

3rd Edition

Anthony J. Bennett
Series editor: Eric Magee

Philip Allan Updates, an imprint of Hodder Education, an Hachette UK company, Market Place, Deddington, Oxfordshire OX15 0SE

Orders

Bookpoint Ltd, 130 Milton Park, Abingdon, Oxfordshire OX14 4SB
tel: 01235 827720
fax: 01235 400454
e-mail: uk.orders@bookpoint.co.uk

Lines are open 9.00 a.m.–5.00 p.m., Monday to Saturday, with a 24-hour message answering service. You can also order through the Philip Allan Updates website:
www.philipallan.co.uk

ISBN 978-0-340-97614-2

First printed 2009

Impression number		5		4		3		2		1	
Year	2014		2013		2012		2011		2010		

Printed in Spain

Hachette UK's policy is to use papers that are natural, renewable and recyclable products and made from wood grown in sustainable forests. The logging and manufacturing processes are expected to conform to the environmental regulations of the country of origin.

P01575

Contents

Introduction 7

Topic 1   The Constitution

A   Before the Constitution 13
      1776–83 • The Philadelphia Convention

B   The Constitution 14
      Introduction • The three compromises • The Constitution in outline • Amending the Constitution

C   Separation of powers 16
      Definition • Explanation

D   Checks and balances 17
      Definition • Explanation • Examples

E   Federalism 18
      Definition • Explanation • Federalism and the Constitution • The development of federalism • Federalism under George W. Bush • The consequences of federalism

Topic 2   Elections and voting

A   Presidential elections 25
      An overview • Primaries • National Party Conventions • The general election campaign • Campaign finance • The media • Election day and the Electoral College • Voting behaviour in presidential elections

B   Congressional elections 46
      An overview • Primaries • Trends in congressional elections

C   Propositions, referendums and recall elections 49

Topic 3   Political parties

A   Party organisation, philosophy, ideology and partisanship 52
      National organisation • State organisation • Philosophy and ideology • Partisanship

B   The two-party system 56
      The facts • The reasons • Other analyses • Theories of party decline • Theories of party renewal

C   Third parties 59
      Types of third parties • Recent success by third parties • Difficulties facing third parties

Topic 4 Pressure groups

A Definition 63

B Types of pressure groups 63

C Functions of pressure groups 64

D Reasons for joining pressure groups 65

E Methods used by pressure groups 65

F Importance of pressure groups 66

G Pressure group activity 67
Environmental protection • Civil rights for African-Americans • Women's rights • Abortion rights • Gun control

H Influence on the federal government 69
Influence on the legislature • Influence on the executive • Influence on the judiciary

I Arguments for and against pressure groups 70

Topic 5 Congress

A Membership 72
Terminology • House membership • Senate membership

B Powers 74
Exclusive powers • Joint powers

C Comparison between the House and the Senate 77

D Leadership 78
Speaker of the House of Representatives • Majority and Minority Leaders

E The committee system 79
Standing committees • House Rules Committee • Conference committees • Select committees

F The legislative process 82
First reading • Committee stage • Timetabling • Second reading • Third reading • Conference committee • Presidential action

G Voting in Congress 85
Political party • Constituents • The administration • Pressure groups • Colleagues and staff • Personal beliefs

H Oversight of the executive branch 89

Topic 6 The presidency

A The powers of the president 91
Propose legislation • Submit the annual budget • Sign legislation • Veto legislation • Act as chief executive • Nominate executive branch officials • Nominate federal judges • Act as commander-in-chief • Negotiate treaties • Pardon

B   The federal bureaucracy.. 97

      Twentieth-century expansion • The size and scale of today's bureaucracy

C   The cabinet... 98

      Definition and membership • Cabinet recruitment • Cabinet meetings • Cabinet councils • Relations with the Executive Office of the President • The cabinet: important or unimportant?

D   The Executive Office of the President.. 102

      Definition and membership • The White House Office • The National Security Council • The Office of Management and Budget

E   Relations with Congress.. 104

      Methods of presidential persuasion • The results of presidential persuasion

F   Limits on presidential power... 107

      Congress • Supreme Court • Public opinion • Pressure groups • The media • The federal bureaucracy • Federalism • Other factors

Topic 7   The vice-presidency

A   Selection, election and powers... 110

      Selection of vice-presidential candidates • Election of the vice-president • Appointment of the vice-president • Constitutional powers

B   The increased importance of the office: why and how............................ 112

      The period of unimportance • The emergence of the 'modern vice-presidency'

Topic 8   The Supreme Court and the protection of rights and liberties

A   The justices... 116

      Membership • Appointment process • Philosophy of justices

B   The power of judicial review.. 118

      Definition and origins • Usage • Political importance

C   The Supreme Court and the protection of rights and liberties.................. 120

      Freedom of religion • Freedom of speech and expression • The right to bear arms • The rights of arrested persons • Capital punishment • The rights of racial minorities • Abortion rights

D   Checks on the Supreme Court... 123

      By Congress • By the president • Other checks

Topic 9   Racial and ethnic politics

A   The civil rights movement... 125

B   Affirmative action... 126

      Brief history • Arguments for and against affirmative action • Has affirmative action been a success?

C   Minority representation in government 128

Minorities in Congress • Minorities and presidential elections • Minorities in the executive branch • Minorities and the judiciary • Minorities in state and local government

D   Protection of rights and liberties of racial and ethnic minorities 130

Topic 10   Key political concepts

A   Accountability 132

B   Authority 133

C   Power 133

D   Democracy 134

E   Representation 135

F   Rights 136

G   Pluralism 136

Answers 138

Introduction

'Those who fail to prepare, should prepare to fail.'

(Abraham Lincoln)

Using revision notes

This is not a textbook. You will doubtless have used one, and hopefully read a good deal of it, making detailed notes from it which you will now have to hand. It is worth stating that this is not a textbook, because it does *not* seek to tell you everything about and explain everything about US politics. You have been taught the course. You have participated in classes. You have read books and articles. You have written essays and exercises. These notes will *not* tell you how to write essays or answer the questions in the examination, but they *will* help you to do yourself justice, to understand better and learn the work you have already done and thus to be successful in the final examinations.

What these revision notes attempt to offer are:
● a concise guide to the main topics and issues
● up-to-date examples, facts and figures
● explanations of the points that might still confuse you
● a structure to help you revise
● some help with preparation for the exam itself

I have written them as if I were talking to the students in my classes, knowing what they find difficult to understand, knowing the mistakes that even the hard-working and well-prepared students can easily make. I have written them having marked literally thousands of essays on US politics, both from my own students and from those across the country as an A-level examiner. I trust what you read here will help you.

Nine of the ten topics covered in these revision notes deal with specific areas of American government and politics. The tenth looks at a number of key political concepts such as democracy, power and representation. It will be important at this level to have a good understanding of these important concepts. It will help you both to understand your American politics better and to make links with the UK government and politics you studied at AS.

Before you start

There are certain things you might need to do *before* you start using these notes. So, ask yourself the following questions:

(1) Have you made sure that the file in which you (hopefully) have kept all your work during this course is well organised? Are all the notes on each topic properly and clearly titled? Are they grouped together under topic headings? (Coloured file dividers are very useful for this.) Have you recently refreshed your memory as to exactly what you've got in the file?

(2) Have you seen copies of past (or example) papers? Do you know the kind of questions you are going to have to answer? Have you grouped questions together under your revision topic headings? (This will help you spot the focus of questions on particular topics.)

(3) Have you subscribed to any journals (such as *Politics Review*) during this course? If you have, have you noted (or highlighted) them, and do you have them in your file? (This will probably mean 'cannibalising' the magazine.)

(4) Have you worked out a revision plan? This means dividing up the course into bite-size pieces, deciding when each is going to be revised so that the revision process is completed well in advance of the examination itself.

If the answer to all these questions is 'yes', keep reading. If not, do it!

How to revise

Students are often told to 'revise'. But do you actually know what that entails? Revision involves a number of tasks:

- **Re-familiarising** yourself with work completed some time ago.
- **Organising** your material into manageable pieces.
- **Learning** the work.

It all takes time so start early, especially on the first two of these tasks. This will help with the third when it becomes time to do that as well.

Once the examination time approaches, you will probably find that classes will finish and you are on your own, often with whole days having to be set aside for revision. Days that you are setting aside for your own revision can be divided into three 3-hour sessions: morning, afternoon, evening. Aim to work for two of them each day. Start early. End early. Get to bed early. You wouldn't be amused if you were asked to sit an exam at midnight. Don't do your revision then either. If you are organised, disciplined and start early enough, it shouldn't be necessary.

For each of these work sessions, set yourself realistic tasks to complete in the allotted time and stick to them. Revision is not just shutting yourself away in a room with a book open in front of you. And as much as possible, write things down. It helps concentration.

Talking of concentration, get those obvious distractions well out of sight and reach: the computer games, the phone (mobile or otherwise), the television, the (non-academic) magazines. If someone disturbs you, tell them (politely) to go away. Decide when — and for how long — you are going to allow yourself a break. (A 10-minute break every hour would not be unreasonable.)

When it comes to committing information to memory, how do you know that you have actually learnt it? The danger here is to mistake what I call 'instant recall' for 'memorising' something. Most of us can instantly repeat something we've just been told. But that does not mean that we have memorised it. (Ever tried remembering someone's phone number the day after they verbally told you what it was?) The recipe for success is to test yourself, first after a few hours, then after a number of hours, then after a day, then after a few days. You will soon see what you can and can't recall. This is why it is so important not to leave this task too late. The parallel I often cite to my students is of the person who goes into the supermarket 5 minutes before closing-time on Christmas Eve to do the entire family shopping. There just isn't time and Christmas lunch is likely to be a fairly disappointing affair in that household. Similarly, your examination results will be a fairly disappointing affair if you don't start early enough and give yourself sufficient time.

What to revise

Over the years, some (unwise) students have sometimes told me after the examination: '*My* questions didn't come up'. I often wondered what they meant. Did they not realise that the exam paper was being set by someone else? Did they imagine they could write the questions as well as the answers? Sadly, of course, only *the examiner's* questions ever come up in an exam. I knew what they meant, of course: 'The (few) topics I revised were not asked'. Tough! They probably didn't learn enough topics. Don't play Russian roulette with your exam chances.

Not only do you need to revise plenty of topics, but you also need to learn more than just facts, as important as they are. Most candidates are going to know the facts. What examiners will be looking for are **up-to-date examples**. So many A-level answers I have marked have contained either no examples at all or ones that were needlessly dated. I didn't, for example, want to see references to the Kennedy/Nixon election of 1960 when the point could just as well be illustrated from the Obama/McCain election of 2008. The other feature that will make your answer stand out is to include some scholarly quotations to back up your argument. This could be something from a noted author on the subject. Even in these revision notes, you will find a few such quotations from people like Richard Neustadt, Richard Fenno and Anthony King. Or it could be a quotation from an article you read in *Politics Review*. Quotations don't need to be long — this is not English literature. Something short and punchy is excellent. So look out for quotations to learn on major topics.

Remember, the recipe for good essays at this level is **logical argument backed up by relevant examples**.

The day of the examination

Here there are a number of rules of thumb:
(1) Arrive in good time — not too early, but certainly not at the last minute.
(2) Have with you everything you need which, for US politics, is likely to mean two pens (black roller-balls are the best) plus anything you need (and are allowed) in the way of bottled water, sweets, cuddly toys or mascots.
(3) Once in the exam room, remind yourself of the length of the exam and the number of questions you have to answer, working out the length of time you can afford on each question (as soon as you can, write down the times when you should be starting your second, third, fourth questions etc.)
(4) Once you are told you may begin, **read every question carefully**.
(5) Quickly rule out those you cannot attempt and decide which to do among those you can.
(6) Plan your answers, deciding the main points you need to make and the order in which you are going to make them.
(7) Keep an eye on the time.
(8) *Never* leave the examination room before the end of the allotted time, even if the rules at your centre allow you to do so.

There is always the temptation for the well-prepared candidate to disadvantage themselves by writing material that is not asked for by the question. It's a kind of 'I know it, so I'm going tell you' mentality. I remember marking an A-level essay which was some nine sides in length. The candidate had been asked the question: 'Why has the US Constitution been subjected to so few amendments?' The main focus I was looking for was the three reasons: the foresight of the founding fathers in writing an adaptable document; the difficulty of the amendment process; and the Supreme Court's ability to make 'interpretative amendments' through its power of judicial review. But this candidate spent pages telling me all about the Philadelphia Convention, the Founding Fathers (complete with biographies on some), as well as detailing the content of virtually all the Articles and Amendments of the Constitution. It was so frustrating. They clearly knew their stuff. They had clearly been well taught and prepared very thoroughly. But it just was *not relevant*.

I sometimes use the analogy that revising for examinations is rather like packing your suitcase to go on a summer holiday. Some people don't pack enough and when the weather turns warm and sunny, they don't have the swimwear or the beach towel that they now wish they had packed. Silly. But others pack everything from raincoat, hat and scarf to swimwear and beach towel. The weather is fine and sunny but it would be such a shame not to wear the raincoat, hat and scarf, having brought them. So while everyone else is strolling along the beach in swimwear, they are sporting the rainwear! Equally silly. Sensible folk will pack more than they need, but not use it. **Sensible candidates will learn more than they need, but not use it.**

Your teacher will doubtless have told you to **'answer the question'**. It sounds so obvious — but it isn't. To ensure that you do this, adopt the following strategy. Before attempting to answer a question ask yourself:

- Is there anything in the question that requires definition, clarification or explanation?
- What is the key word or phrase of the question?

You will often need to begin your answer by defining, clarifying or explaining things. For example, imagine you are responding to the question: 'Examine the claim that the process for selecting presidential candidates is undemocratic'. Well, what is 'the process for selecting presidential candidates?' You will need to explain. And what does the word 'undemocratic' mean? You will need to clarify. Only then can you answer the question.

Whatever you identify as the 'key word or phrase' of the question should be used as the focus for your answer. So in the example just given, the key word is 'undemocratic'. The best answers will be organised along the following lines:

(1) An explanation of 'the process for selecting presidential candidates'.
(2) A definition/clarification of the term 'undemocratic'.
(3) Arguments to support the claim.
(4) Arguments against the claim.

There is absolutely no doubt that an essay written according to this plan will answer the question.

Revision notes structure

These notes have been structured into ten topics as follows:

- Topic 1   The Constitution
- Topic 2   Elections and voting
- Topic 3   Political parties
- Topic 4   Pressure groups
- Topic 5   Congress
- Topic 6   The presidency
- Topic 7   The vice-presidency
- Topic 8   The Supreme Court and the protection of rights and liberties
- Topic 9   Racial and ethnic politics
- Topic 10   Key political concepts

These topics are then further divided as follows:

- Main headings **A** **B** **C**
- Subdivisions *1* *2* *3*
- Subdivided again 1.1 1.2 1.3
- Subdivided yet again **1.1a** **1.1b** **1.1c**

Each page is split into two columns. On the right you will find the main body of the text and tables. On the left you will find 'comments' that should help you understand the text and avoid common errors and misunderstandings. Topics 1–9 also contain questions to test your knowledge and understanding and help reinforce your learning. Answers are provided at the end of the book.

Acknowledgements

I owe a considerable debt to my former students at Charterhouse over many years, not only for their unfailing enthusiasm but also for their patience as I tried out my ideas on them. But whilst the credit is shared, the blame for any errors which remain is mine alone. 'The buck stops here!' Good luck!

Anthony J. Bennett

TOPIC 1 The Constitution

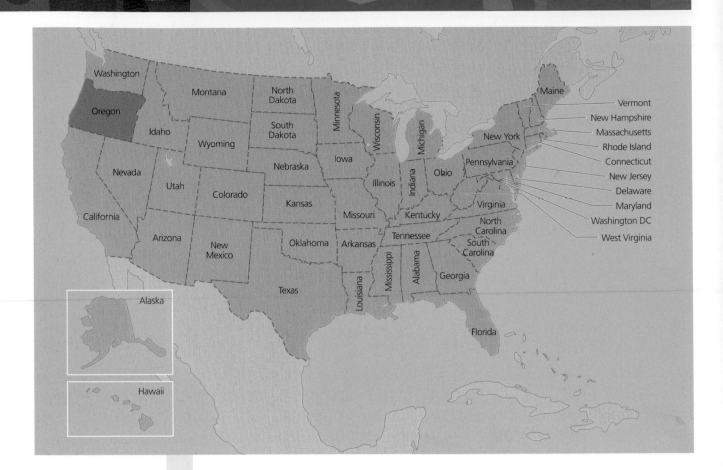

Shaded in the map above.

In order to understand fully the government and politics of the USA, you will need to have some comprehension of how the nation was formed and how the Constitution came to be written in 1787. You will also need to understand the basic principles that underlie the Constitution — **separation of powers, checks and balances**, and **federalism**. Remember that the USA is a vast country. You can fit the entire UK into Oregon. Even the 48 contiguous states — not counting Alaska and Hawaii — encompass over 3,000 miles (4,800 kilometres) and four time zones. It's as far from New York to Los Angeles as it is from New York to London. When it's midday in London and 7 a.m. in New York, it's still only 4 a.m. in California. **Vastness** is one characteristic of America. **Diversity** is another, diversity in terms of race, culture, language, religion, climate and economy. The USA needs a particular kind of governmental and political structure to cope with all this.

The topic is divided into the following five major headings:

A Before the Constitution

B The Constitution

C Separation of powers

D Checks and balances

E Federalism

A Before the Constitution

1 *1776–83*

You don't need to know the details of American history for this course in government and politics, but it helps to have a working knowledge of what came before the founding of the USA. The order in which things happened is more important than the dates themselves.

Here is a very brief survey of what occurred in the years before the writing of the American Constitution:

- **1776:** the 13 colonies on the eastern seaboard of North America declared their independence from Great Britain in the **Declaration of Independence**.
- **1776–83:** there followed the **War of Independence** between the former colonies and Great Britain.
- **1781:** the newly independent colonies decided to establish a **confederacy** — a loose association of states in which almost all political power rests with the individual states — by the **Articles of Confederation**.

Between 1781 and 1787 there was almost no national government. Virtually all power resided with the states. Virginians ruled Virginia. New Yorkers ruled New York, and so on. That was what they had fought to gain from Britain. There was no president. There was no national court. There was a Congress, but it could not pass any laws; it was merely a debating chamber. The states squabbled with each other, principally over trade (taxes charged by each state for goods to pass through) and money (each state had its own currency). Chaos ensued.

To help bring order out of chaos, the **Philadelphia Convention** convened in the summer of 1787.

2 *The Philadelphia Convention*

Rhode Island delegates were fearful that the hard-won gains of the War of Independence would be lost and refused to attend.

At this time, Virginia was the state with the largest population.

Again, all you need to know here are the basic facts:
- It was convened in Philadelphia on 25 May 1787.
- Delegates from the 13 states were invited.
- 55 of the invited 74 turned up — Rhode Island was the only state to send no delegates.
- It was presided over by **George Washington**.
- Also present were James Madison, Thomas Jefferson and Alexander Hamilton.
- Although the stated purpose of the Convention was merely to **revise** the Articles of Confederation, they decided to scrap them and write a new Constitution.
- Divisions arose between the small-population and large-population states.
- The Virginia Plan set out the wishes of the large-population states.
- The New Jersey Plan set out those of the small-population states.
- The Connecticut Compromise (often called 'the Great Compromise') provided the basis for agreement.
- The new Constitution was written by these 55 delegates, who became known as the Founding Fathers.

B The Constitution

1 Introduction

This is where your knowledge and understanding need to become much more detailed.

The Founding Fathers decided to write a new Constitution. This involved making a whole number of **compromises**. Indeed, 'compromise' is a key word to aid full understanding of American government and politics. The Constitution is made up of a whole series of compromises, and to govern — whether you are the president or a member of Congress — involves making compromises. That is what the Founding Fathers wanted. Alistair Cooke has written that the American Constitution was founded upon three great principles: 'compromise, compromise and compromise'.

This is the kind of 'scholarly quotation' you ought to try and get into an essay. Short but insightful.

Here are three of the major compromises embodied in the new Constitution.

2 The three compromises

2.1 The form of government

Under Great Britain, the colonies had been ruled under a **unitary** form of government. All political power rested with Great Britain, none with the colonies themselves. The colonists disliked this. As we have just seen, from 1781 they had been ruled by a **confederal** form of government where virtually all political power rested with the individual states, very little with the national government. This had simply not worked. The compromise was to devise a new form of government — a **federal** form of government. This gives some political power to the national (or federal) government but other, equally important, powers to the state governments.

Notice 'equally important' — not just trivial matters such as keeping the roads clean.

2.2 The representation of the states

In the new Congress, the large-population states wanted representation to be proportional to population. The bigger the population of a state, the more representatives it would have in the new Congress. The small-population states wanted equal representation. The compromise was to have a Congress made up of two houses — the House of Representatives and the Senate. In the House of Representatives, there would be representation proportional to population. In the Senate, there would be equal representation for all states, regardless of population.

'Bicameral' is the technical phrase — made up of two houses or 'chambers'.

Don't use the phrase 'proportional representation'; it isn't.

2.3 The choosing of the president

There were many different suggestions about how to choose the president. Some thought the president should be **appointed**. Others thought the president should be **directly elected** by the people. The compromise was to have the president **indirectly elected** by an Electoral College (see Topic 2.A.7.2). The people would elect the Electoral College and the 'Electors' within the Electoral College would choose the president.

'Electors' with a capital 'E' to avoid misunderstanding.

3 The Constitution in outline

You should be familiar with the first three Articles of the Constitution:
- Article I: established that **the Congress** was to be made up of two chambers; laid down methods of election, terms of office and powers (see Topic 5).
- Article II: established **a President of the USA**; laid down methods of election, terms of office and powers (see Topic 6).
- Article III: established the **United States Supreme Court**; laid down the judges' terms of office and their jurisdiction (see Topic 8).

Attached to the first seven Articles were ten Amendments known as **the Bill of Rights**. You should be familiar with Amendments I, II, V, VIII and X.

4 Amending the Constitution

Amending the Constitution is a two-stage process: **proposal** and **ratification** (see Table 1.1).

(1) **Proposals to amend** the Constitution can be made either by Congress with a **two-thirds majority** in favour in **both houses**, or by a national Constitutional Convention called at the request of two-thirds of the state legislatures. The latter has never been used.

(2) **Ratification** can be made either by **three-quarters of the state legislatures** or by three-quarters of the states holding a Constitutional Convention. The latter has been used only once — to ratify the 21st Amendment in 1933.

> Note that this three-quarters figure concerns the proportion of states that must ratify, not the majority by which they must ratify the Amendment.

Amendments proposed by:	Amendments ratified by:
Either **Congress:** two-thirds majority in both houses required or **National Constitutional Convention:** called by at least two-thirds of the states (never used)	Either **State legislatures:** three-quarters of the state legislatures must vote to ratify, often within a stated time limit or **State Constitutional Conventions:** three-quarters of the states must hold Conventions and vote to ratify

Table 1.1 Procedures for amending the Constitution

Following the ratification of the Bill of Rights in 1791, there have been 17 further amendments in around 220 years. Two of these 17 cancel each other out: the 18th and 21st Amendments imposing and then ending the prohibition of alcohol.

Numerous amendments have been proposed but not ratified. Recent examples include proposals to:
- guarantee equal rights for women
- require the federal government to pass a balanced budget
- impose term limits on members of Congress
- forbid desecration of the American flag

Between 1995 and 2008, Congress voted 23 times on constitutional amendments — 17 times in the House, six times in the Senate. The House passed amendments on seven occasions, six being on the same amendment — to forbid flag desecration. But the Senate rejected every amendment it considered during this time, including the Balanced Budget Amendment in three successive years — 1995, 1996 and 1997 — and flag desecration in 1995, 2000 and 2006.

Subjects
Balanced budget
Congressional term limits
Flag desecration
Tax limitation
School prayers
Super-majority to raise taxes
Marriage protection

Table 1.2 Subjects of constitutional amendments introduced in Congress, 1995–2008

So, why has the constitution been so rarely amended? There are five main reasons:

(1) The Founding Fathers created a deliberately difficult amendment process.
(2) The vagueness of the Constitution, which has allowed the document to evolve without the need for constant formal amendment.
(3) The Supreme Court's power of judicial review, which allows the Court to amend the meaning of the Constitution while the words remain largely unaltered (see Topic 8).
(4) The reverence with which the Constitution is regarded, which makes many politicians cautious of tampering with it.
(5) The experience of the 18th Amendment, regarding the prohibition of alcohol, which was repealed (by the 21st Amendment) just 14 years later.

C Separation of powers

Watch for spelling of 'separation'. 'Legisla*ture*' is the noun; 'legisla*tive*' is the adjective. Don't confuse the two. It is 'the legislature' or 'the legislative branch'.

1 Definition

The separation of powers is a theory of government by which power is divided between three branches of government — the legislature, the executive and the judiciary — each acting both independently and interdependently.

2 Explanation

'Executing' means 'carrying out'.

The functions of government can be divided into three:
(1) Legislating: this is done by the **legislature** which **makes the laws**.
(2) Executing: this is done by the **executive** which **carries out the laws**.
(3) Enforcing: this is done by the **judiciary**, which **enforces the laws**. The judiciary also **interprets the laws** and, in the USA, where there is a written Constitution, **interprets the Constitution** (the 'supreme law').

Branch	Function	Body
The legislature	Makes the laws	Congress
The executive	Carries out the laws	The president and the federal bureaucracy
The judiciary	Enforces and interprets the laws	The Supreme Court and the Appeal and Trial Courts

Table 1.3 The three branches of government

But the functions are not completely separated. Indeed, the term 'separation of powers' is rather confusing for it is not the 'powers' that are separate but the institutions. As Richard Neustadt has stated: 'The Constitutional Convention of 1787 is supposed to have created a government of "separated powers". It did nothing of the sort. Rather, it created a government of **separated institutions sharing powers**.' So the theory is more accurately described as a theory of **'shared powers'** than 'separated powers'. The institutions — the Congress, the presidency and the courts — are indeed separate. The personnel of these three branches are separate. In 2009, Senator Barack Obama had to resign from the Senate in order to become president. So did Senator Joe Biden in order to become vice-president. So did Senators Hillary Clinton and Ken Salazar in order to become members of President Obama's cabinet. The personnel and the institutions are separate, but their powers are shared. This sharing of powers is what is called **'checks and balances'**.

> This is a most important paragraph. Make sure you understand it fully.
>
> Another of those 'scholarly quotations' for your essays.

D Checks and balances

1 Definition

Checks and balances is a theory of government by which each of the three branches of government — the legislature, the executive and the judiciary — exercise checks upon the powers and actions of the others.

2 Explanation

> Professor S. E. Finer likened the president and Congress to 'two halves of a bank note, each useless without the other'.

Think of the government's three branches of government as a bank note cut into three pieces. Each is useless without the others but together they are useful. On their own, the Congress, the president and the Supreme Court can do little or nothing. To get things done, they must **cooperate**. That is what the Founding Fathers wanted, to avoid too much power being vested in one branch. It would thus avoid what they most feared, which was tyranny. The Founding Fathers were especially worried about the president becoming something of a tyrant, so they subjected the executive branch to the most comprehensive set of checks. Also keep in mind that the checks and balances between the legislature and the executive (the Congress and the president) can become even more complicated when these two branches are controlled by different political parties. In the period from January 1969 to January 2009, for only 10 ½ of the 40 years did the same party control both branches of government. This can lead to **gridlock**, a term derived from traffic jams in American cities where the intersections of their grid-patterned streets become jammed and as a result nothing can move.

3 Examples

These are laid out in Table 1.4.

Checks on → Checks by ↓	The legislature	The executive	The judiciary
The legislature		• Amend/delay/reject the president's legislation • Override the president's veto • Control of the budget • Senate's power to confirm numerous appointments made by the president • Senate's power to ratify treaties negotiated by the president • Declare war • Investigation • Impeachment, trial, conviction and removal from office of any member of the executive branch, including the president	• Senate's power to confirm appointments made by the president • Initiate constitutional amendments • Impeachment, trial, conviction and removal from office of any member of the judiciary
The executive	• Recommend legislation • Veto legislation • Call Congress into special session		• Appointment of judges • Pardon
The judiciary	• Judicial review: the power to declare Acts of Congress unconstitutional	• Judicial review: the power to declare actions of any member of the executive branch — including the president — unconstitutional	

Table 1.4 Checks and balances

E Federalism

1 Definition

'Substantive jurisdiction' = important powers.

Federalism is a theory of government by which power is divided between a national government and state governments, each having their own areas of substantive jurisdiction.

2 | *Explanation*

Federalism involves a certain level of **decentralisation**. As already explained, it is a compromise between a highly centralised form of government on the one hand and a loose confederation of independent states on the other. In other words, it is a compromise between the two experiences America had before 1787 — government by Great Britain and government by the Articles of Confederation. It is a very appropriate form of government for a country as large and diverse as the USA. It allows for both national unity as well as regional and local diversity.

3 | *Federalism and the Constitution*

Nowhere are the words 'federal' or 'federalism' to be found in the American Constitution. How, then, is it written into this document?

- By Articles I, II and III, which lay out the powers of the national government.
- By Amendment X, which guarantees that all the remaining powers 'are reserved to the states and to the people'.

It is important to remember the political atmosphere in which the Constitution was drawn up. The former British colonies had successfully got rid of what they saw as the distant, autocratic and highly centralised government of Great Britain. They had then tried to allow each of the individual states to govern themselves, but this had resulted in chaos. So the new Constitution had somehow to square the circle. It had to 'form a more perfect Union' — that is, provide some central authority — and also to protect the interests of the individual states. So the Constitution had to do a number of potentially conflicting things at once:

- It had to give certain **exclusive powers** to the new national (federal) government. Only the national government could coin money, negotiate treaties, tax imports and exports or maintain troops in peacetime.
- It had to offer guarantees of **states' rights**. So, for example, the states were guaranteed equal representation in the Senate, that their borders would not be changed without their consent and that the Constitution could not be amended without the agreement of three-quarters of them.
- It had to make clear that there were also **states' responsibilities**. Each state had to recognise the laws of each other state by, for example, returning fugitives.

All this the Constitution did. But what it failed to do — and wisely so — was to lay down any definite line between the **concurrent powers** of the national and state governments. This has meant that the concept of federalism has been able to develop over the subsequent two centuries. Although, for example, in Article I Congress was given specific powers to 'coin money', 'declare war' and 'raise and support armies', it was also given the power 'to provide for the common defense and general welfare of the United States'. And it was also given the

An extract from the opening sentence of the Preamble to the Constitution: 'We the people, in order to form...'.

power to 'make all laws which shall be necessary and proper for carrying into execution the foregoing powers'. This latter clause of Article I is known as the **elastic clause** of the Constitution, as it has allowed the powers of the national government to be stretched a good deal since 1787.

4 The development of federalism

Federalism is not a fixed concept; it is ever changing. As America has changed, so has the concept of federalism.

The most significant changes that have occurred in the USA since 1787 and have led to the development and evolution of federalism are:
- westward expansion
- the growth in population
- industrialisation
- improvements in communication — by road, rail and air, as well as by post, telephone, radio, television, fax and e-mail
- America's foreign policy role and world-power status

During the latter part of the nineteenth century and the first two-thirds of the twentieth century, all these five factors led to an increased role for the federal government and a decline in the power of state governments. But during the final third of the twentieth century, there was a distinct move in the opposite direction as Americans wanted to see more power and more decisions devolved to the states wherever this was possible. It is therefore possible to discern three distinct phases of federalism in America:

> Dates are deliberately vague. Avoid being too precise. These were gradual changes.

(1) **Dual federalism** (1780s–1920s) — an era in which the state governments had significant power.
(2) **Cooperative federalism** (1930s–60s) — an era in which the federal government became more and more powerful, sometimes at the expense of the states. This is associated with the Democratic Presidents Franklin Roosevelt ('The New Deal'), Truman ('The Fair Deal'), Kennedy ('The New Frontier') and Johnson ('The Great Society'), as well as the USA becoming a world power. The federal government administered **categorical grants**, schemes by which Washington was able to stipulate how federal tax dollars were used by the states.
(3) **New federalism** (1970s–present) — an era in which, wherever possible, power was devolved to the states. This is associated with the Republican Presidents Nixon, Ford, Reagan and George Bush, but was also partly adopted by Clinton in the 1990s. The federal government gradually moved towards **block grants** and **revenue-sharing**, by which Washington allowed the states greater independence in how federal tax dollars were spent.

> President Clinton famously remarked (1996): 'The era of big government is over.'

As a result of policies pursued by administrations of both parties — though especially Republicans — over the last 30 years, the states have seen quite a significant increase in their autonomy and power. Decentralisation and states' rights are once again the buzz words in American politics. This has come about through a number of important developments:
- The reduction of federal government economic aid to the states.
- A perception that the federal government programmes such as FDR's New

Deal and Johnson's Great Society had not been as successful as at first thought.

- A belief that the federal government had simply failed to tackle some pressing social problems such as those associated with gun crime, drugs, abortion, welfare and poverty.
- This led to a widespread distrust and scepticism of the federal government and 'Washington politicians'.
- Decisions by the mainly Republican-appointed Supreme Court, which began to limit the scope of the federal government in such cases as *United States v. Lopez* (1995) and *Printz v. United States* (1997) while upholding states' rights in such cases as *Webster v. Reproductive Health Services* (1989) and *Planned Parenthood of Southeastern Pennsylvania v. Casey* (1992) (see Topic 8.C for details).
- The Republican domination of the White House during the 1970s and 1980s, and again during the first 8 years of this century, and control of Congress between 1995 and 2006, which allowed conservative politicians to push their states' rights agenda.
- The election of a significant number of Republican state governors during the 1990s, which led to state-based innovations in such states as New Jersey (under Governor Christine Todd Whitman) and Wisconsin (under Governor Tommy Thompson).

5 *Federalism under George W. Bush*

You would expect a Republican president to be keen on decentralisation and giving more power to the state governments. You would certainly expect that of a Republican president who had been a state governor such as George W. Bush, who was governor of Texas for 6 years before entering the White House. But that wasn't what happened. During the presidency of George W. Bush (2001–09), federal government spending grew at a rate not seen since the days of President Johnson in the 1960s — and he was a Democrat. Whereas former Republican presidents had arrived in Washington determined to cut federal government bureaucracy, George W. Bush expanded it.

There are five particular reasons for this expansion of the federal government under George W. Bush:
(1) the war in Iraq
(2) homeland security issues following the attacks on the US on 9/11 (2001)
(3) the expansion of the Medicare programme
(4) the No Child Left Behind Act passed by Congress in 2001
(5) the Wall Street and banking collapse of 2008

Not all Republicans agreed with Bush's huge expansion of federal government spending. Even some of his own party derided such programmes as '**big-government conservatism**'. Bush was widely criticised by many conservative Republicans for not vetoing expensive federal government programmes. Bush failed to use a single veto during his entire first term (2001–05), the first president to do so since Martin van Buren between 1837 and 1841.

Bush was also criticised for what many saw as the federal government's somewhat feeble initial response to the devastation caused by Hurricane Katrina in 2005.

Finally, when in 2008 the Bush White House authorised the secretary of the treasury, Henry Paulson, to take control of the two troubled, privately-owned but government-sponsored mortgage companies — known colloquially as Fannie Mae and Freddie Mac — there was more criticism heaped on President Bush, by conservative Republicans in particular. This was followed by a Bush White House-sponsored $700 billion so-called 'bail out' package for Wall Street to alleviate the effects of the credit crunch. The legislation passed through Congress but with mainly Democrat votes.

In 1996 Bill Clinton had commented that the era of big government was over. By the end of the George W. Bush administration, it was clear that it was back.

6 *The consequences of federalism*

You should be aware of the way in which federalism affects so many aspects of US government and politics. Here are a few important ways:

- Tremendous variation in state laws concerning such matters as the age at which one can marry, drive a car and must attend school.
- Variation in penalties for law-breaking from state to state.
- Complexity of the American legal system, having both national and state courts.
- Each state not only has its own laws and courts but its own Constitution.
- Complexity of the tax system: income tax (federal and state); state property taxes; local sales taxes.

See Topic 2.

- All elections in the USA are state-based, run largely under state law.
- The frequency and number of elections.

See Topic 3.
See Topic 6.

- Political parties are decentralised and largely state-based.
- Regional diversity (the South, the Midwest, the Northeast etc.) and regional considerations when making appointments to, for example, the cabinet, or when 'balancing the ticket' in the presidential election.

Article	Content	Ratified
I	The powers etc. of the legislature	1787
II	The powers etc. of the executive	1787
III	The powers etc. of the judiciary	1787
IV	Federal–state and state–state relationships	1787
V	Amendment procedures	1787
VI	Miscellaneous	1787
VII	Ratification procedure for the Constitution	1787

Amendment	Content	Ratified
I	Freedom of religion, press, speech, assembly	1791
II	Right to bear arms	1791
III	Privacy of property owners	1791
IV	Freedom from unreasonable searches and seizures	1791

V	Rights of accused persons; due process clause	1791
VI	Rights when on trial	1791
VII	Common-law suits	1791
VIII	Prohibition of excessive bail and 'cruel and unusual' punishments	1791
IX	Reserved rights to the people	1791
X	Reserved rights to the states	1791
XI	Limits of judicial power	1795
XII	Revision of Electoral College procedure	1804
XIII	Prohibition of slavery	1865
XIV	Guarantee of 'equal protection' for all; 'due process' clause applied to the states	1868
XV	Blacks given voting rights	1870
XVI	Congress given power to tax incomes	1913
XVII	Direct election of Senators	1913
[XVIII]	[Prohibition of alcohol]	1919
XIX	Women given voting rights	1920
XX	Presidential and congressional terms to begin in January	1933
XXI	Repealed 18th Amendment	1933
XXII	Two-term limit for the president	1951
XXIII	Washington DC given voting rights in presidential elections	1961
XXIV	Poll tax prohibited as requirement for voting	1964
XXV	Presidential disability and succession	1967
XXVI	Voting age lowered to 18	1971
XXVII	Limits on timing of congressional pay rises	1992

Table 1.5 The Constitution in brief

Questions

1 Define the following systems of government: **(a)** unitary; **(b)** confederal; **(c)** federal.

2 What do Articles I, II and III of the federal Constitution deal with?

3 What majority in both houses of Congress is required to make a constitutional amendment?

4 What proportion of the states is then required to ratify a constitutional amendment?

5 Define the separation of powers.

6 Explain in a short phrase the function of each of the three branches of government.

7 Complete the following quotation by Richard Neustadt: 'the Constitutional Convention of 1787 created a government of…' (4 words).

8 Define checks and balances.

9 In relation to federalism, define the following terms: **(a)** exclusive powers; **(b)** concurrent powers.

10 Complete the following quotation by Bill Clinton, which he made in 1996: 'the era of big government…' (2 words).

11 Give five reasons why the federal government expanded during George W. Bush's presidency.

Elections and voting

Even the UK media cover quite a bit about US presidential elections. But that does not necessarily mean that we — or they — fully understand what is going on. There are numerous things over which confusion readily occurs. From a glance at the media coverage on this side of the Atlantic, it would be tempting to think that there were no other elections in the USA. Far from it. There are elections for both houses of Congress as well as elections at state and local level for governors, state legislators, city mayors and a host of other elected officials. And then at the state level there are also propositions, referendums and recall elections. We shall try to establish what happens, why people vote as they do and the role that the media and money play in the whole electoral process in the USA.

The topic is divided into the following three major headings:

A Presidential elections

B Congressional elections

C Propositions, referendums and recall elections

A Presidential elections

1 An overview

Presidential elections occur:

- every 4 years
- in years divisible by four: 2000, 2004, 2008, 2012 etc.
- on the Tuesday after the first Monday in November (i.e. between 2 November and 8 November)

The Constitution (Article II) states that to be eligible to be president a person must:

- be a natural-born US citizen
- be at least 35 years of age
- have been resident in the USA for at least 14 years

The Constitution (Amendment XXII, passed in 1951) also states that a person cannot serve more than two terms as president.

A presidential election can be thought of as occurring in **four** stages. The first two are concerned with **choosing the candidates**; the second two are concerned with **electing the president**. (See Table 2.1 on page 26.)

So if 1 November is a Tuesday, the presidential election is on 8 November.

In other words, born as a US citizen.

This is why George W. Bush could not be a candidate for president in 2008 and can never be again.

In exam questions do be careful to see the difference between the phrases 'selecting presidential candidates' and 'electing the president'.

Stage	Functions	Occurs
1. Primaries and caucuses	(i) Show popularity of candidates (ii) Choose delegates to attend the National Party Conventions	Early January–early June
2. National Party Conventions	(i) Choose presidential candidate (ii) Choose vice-presidential candidate (iii) Decide on party platform	July–August /early September (each lasts 4 days)
3. General election campaign	The campaign between candidates of the various parties	September, October, first week of November
4. Election day and Electoral College votes	Elect the president and vice-president through the Electoral College	Election day: Tuesday after the first Monday in November Electoral College votes: Monday after the second Wednesday in December

Table 2.1 Presidential elections: a four-stage process

2 *Primaries*

2.1 Definitions

A **presidential primary** is an election to select a party's candidate for the presidency. Some states with a small population spread over a large geographic area often hold **caucuses** instead of a primary. The states that held caucuses rather than a primary in 2008 included Iowa, Wyoming, North Dakota, Minnesota and Nevada.

A caucus is a series of meetings to select a party's candidate for the presidency.

2.2 Functions

Presidential primaries have two main functions:
(1) To show the popularity of presidential candidates; primaries can therefore be thought of as political 'beauty contests'.
(2) To choose delegates to go to the National Party Conventions.

2.3 How primaries are run

In answers, having quickly made the distinction between primaries and caucuses, you can use the term 'primaries', as that is what the vast majority of states hold nowadays.

Presidential primaries are run under **state** law, not federal law. That means there are potentially 50 different ways of running primaries, which is very confusing. Just keep to the main rules of thumb. You need to know that states decide **six** important things about primaries:
(1) **Whether to hold a primary or a caucus.** The vast majority of states now hold primaries.
(2) **When to hold the primary.** Primaries tend to be held between early January and early June. But each state will decide exactly when within that 4–5-month period to schedule their primary: whether to go early or late, to go for a date on their own or to coincide it with other, maybe neighbouring, states.
(3) **How to conduct the primary.** Recently, some states have experimented with postal voting and even electronic voting via the Internet.
(4) **Who exactly can vote in the primary.** It is important to understand that any registered voter can vote in a primary in any state. But in some states,

In the USA, unlike the UK, you have to take the initiative to go and register to vote.

Notice this is no more than saying you are a Democrat or a Republican. It does not require you to be a paid-up, card-carrying party member.

Again, don't use the term 'proportional representation'; it isn't.

when you register you are asked to declare your party affiliation — whether you consider yourself to be a Democrat or Republican. Some states then allow only registered Democrats to vote in the Democratic primary and only registered Republicans to vote in the Republican primary. This is known as a **closed primary**. Other states don't bother with establishing party affiliation. They allow any registered voter to decide, on the day of the primary, whether they want to vote in the Democratic primary or the Republican primary. This is known as an **open primary**.

(5) **Who can be on the ballot.** States have their own laws about who gets on the ballot. In some states, notably New York, these are very strange indeed and often keep serious, well-known candidates off the ballot.

(6) **How to allocate the delegates.** In most primaries, candidates are awarded delegates in proportion to the votes they get. This is known as a **proportional primary**. Most states set a **threshold** — a minimum percentage of votes a candidate must receive to get any of that state's delegates. The threshold is usually 15% of the vote. However, in some Republican primaries, whoever gets the most votes wins all that state's delegates to the National Party Convention. This is known as a **winner-takes-all primary**. The Democratic Party forbids them, so all their primaries are proportional primaries.

Candidate	Votes	Percentage	Delegates
Barack Obama	295,091	55.4	25
Hillary Clinton	141,128	26.5	12
John Edwards	93,552	17.8	8
Bill Richardson	725	0.1	0
Joseph Biden	693	0.1	0

Table 2.2 A proportional primary: the South Carolina Democratic primary, 2008

Candidate	Votes	Percentage	Delegates
John McCain	333,001	51.8	87
Mitt Romney	178,043	27.7	0
Mike Huckabee	68,477	10.7	0
Ron Paul	40,113	6.2	0
Rudy Giuliani	23,260	3.6	0

Table 2.3 A winner-takes-all primary: the New York Republican primary, 2008

2.4 The growth in importance of primaries

Nowadays the presidential primaries are very important. They are really the only route to becoming the presidential nominee of a major party. But that was not always the case. Until 1968, most states did not hold either primaries or caucuses. Candidates might enter a few or none of the primaries. Decisions were made not by **registered voters in primaries or caucuses** but rather by **state party officials in State Party Conventions**. These were the so-called 'smoke-filled rooms'. They were dominated by important state party officials such as state governors, city mayors or state party chairmen. These were the so-called 'party bosses'. The system was undemocratic and often corrupt.

In 1968, the Democratic presidential nomination went to Vice-President Hubert Humphrey, who had not entered a single primary. Supporters of Senator Eugene McCarthy, who had entered a number of that year's 18 Democratic primaries and caucuses, were angry. After Humphrey lost the November election, the Democrats set up the **McGovern–Fraser Commission** to draw up new rules for selecting future presidential nominees. This Commission recommended that:

- all states should hold either primaries or caucuses (primaries being preferred, as they are a secret ballot and attract a larger turn-out)
- all delegates should be chosen in these primaries and caucuses
- delegates should be representative — in terms of gender, race and age — of their state parties

This is why they also affected the Republican Party.

These reforms were implemented by **changes in state laws** in readiness for the 1972 presidential election. Ever since then, primaries have grown in number and importance. Nowadays, anyone who wants to be seriously considered for the presidential nomination of either the Democratic or Republican party must enter the primaries and caucuses, because it is there that the vast majority of delegates are won. And it is the delegates who finally choose the candidate.

2.5 Front-loading

As primaries have become more and more important, states have tried to make their primary more prominent and influential by moving the date earlier in the year. This is called **'front-loading'**. The number of states holding their primaries or caucuses before the end of March increased from just 11 in 1980 to 42 by 2008. And those 42 states included the eight largest states — New York, Texas, California, Florida, Illinois, Michigan, Pennsylvania and Ohio. California had moved from early June in 1980 to early February in 2008. New York had moved from mid-April to early February. By 5 February 2008, 55% of the delegates to the Democratic and Republican Conventions had already been chosen.

2.6 The invisible primary

This front-loading has increased the importance of another phenomenon — the **invisible primary**. The so-called invisible primary begins almost immediately after the previous presidential election and lasts through to the holding of the first primary and caucus of the election year. It is called 'invisible' because no scheduled event is held during this period. There is therefore nothing to see. It is a time when would-be candidates try to get 'mentioned' in the serious press — newspapers like the *Washington Post* and the *New York Times* — or on television programmes like *The News Hour with Jim Lehrer* on PBS or *Inside Politics* on CNN. It is during this time that candidates will set up exploratory committees and then, eventually, announce formally that they are running for the presidential nomination of their party. It is also an important time for fundraising.

The News Hour with Jim Lehrer is a US equivalent of the BBC's *Newsnight*.

Because the primary season itself is now so short — in 2004 both George W. Bush and John Kerry had made certain of their party's nomination by 2 March —

there is no longer any time to build name recognition, momentum and money during the primaries. So one has to do it *before* — during the invisible primary.

This means campaigns start much earlier. For example:
- **1960:** Senator John F. Kennedy announced he was running for the presidency on 2 January of that year, **66 days** before the first primary.
- **2008:** Senator Barack Obama announced he was running for the presidency **332 days** before the first primary.

There is also much evidence to suggest that this is a most important stage. For example:
- Since 1968, the Republicans have nominated as their candidate the person who was ahead in the opinion polls at the end of the invisible primary on 10 out of 11 occasions (see Table 2.4).
- Since 1968, the Democrats have nominated as their candidate the person who was ahead in the opinion polls at the end of the invisible primary on only 6 of those 11 occasions (see Table 2.5).

2.7 Advantages of primaries

The new system of selecting presidential candidates, introduced as a result of the McGovern–Fraser reforms, has a number of advantages:
- Increased level of participation by ordinary voters — 30% In 2008.
- Increased level of interest — as witnessed in the Democratic nomination race in 2008.
- Increased choice of candidates — up to 14 candidates in 2008.
- Opening up of the process to 'outsider' candidates such as Jimmy Carter (1976), Bill Clinton (1992) and Barack Obama (2008).
- Removing the power of the party bosses.
- Significantly diminishing opportunities for corruption by doing away with the old 'smoke-filled rooms'.
- Weeding out candidates not up to the gruelling contest, such as Paul Tsongas of Massachusetts in 1992, who had been diagnosed with cancer in the 1980s.

2.8 Disadvantages of primaries

This reformed system has a number of identifiable disadvantages:
- Turnout is usually low — less than 20% of eligible voters, though 30% in 2008.
- Voters who do vote are unrepresentative of typical general election voters — more elderly, more ideological, better educated and more wealthy.
- It makes the whole selection process far too long, which may discourage some better-qualified candidates from running.
- It is too expensive.
- It is too media-dominated.
- Bitter personal battles can develop, for example George Bush v. Patrick Buchanan in the 1992 Republican primaries, and to some extent between Hillary Clinton and Barack Obama in the 2008 Democratic primaries.
- It fails to test a number of important presidential qualities.
- It lacks significant input by professional politicians, with too much power being given to ordinary voters — lacks 'peer review'.

This was certainly the case in the Democratic primaries in 2008 during the race between Barack Obama and Hillary Clinton.

Use the term 'more ideological' rather than 'extremist'. The latter overstates the point as well as having overtones of disapproval.

Your 'peers' being your 'equals' — those who supposedly know you best.

Year	Republican presidential candidate ahead in opinion polls before the New Hampshire primary	Republican candidate eventually nominated for the presidency
1968	Richard Nixon	Richard Nixon
1972	Richard Nixon	Richard Nixon
1976	Gerald Ford	Gerald Ford
1980	Ronald Reagan	Ronald Reagan
1984	Ronald Reagan	Ronald Reagan
1988	George H.W. Bush	George H.W. Bush
1992	George H.W. Bush	George H.W. Bush
1996	Bob Dole	Bob Dole
2000	George W. Bush	George W. Bush
2004	George W. Bush	George W. Bush
2008	Rudy Giuliani	John McCain

Table 2.4 Republican presidential candidates: ahead in opinion polls before the New Hampshire primary and eventually nominated, 1968–2008

Year	Democratic presidential candidate ahead in opinion polls before the New Hampshire primary	Democratic candidate eventually nominated for the presidency
1968	Lyndon Johnson	Hubert Humphrey
1972	Hubert Humphrey	George McGovern
1976	Jimmy Carter	Jimmy Carter
1980	Jimmy Carter	Jimmy Carter
1984	Walter Mondale	Walter Mondale
1988	Gary Hart	Michael Dukakis
1992	Bill Clinton	Bill Clinton
1996	Bill Clinton	Bill Clinton
2000	Al Gore	Al Gore
2004	Howard Dean	John Kerry
2008	Hillary Clinton	Barack Obama

Table 2.5 Democratic presidential candidates: ahead in opinion polls before the New Hampshire primary and eventually nominated, 1968–2008

2.9 Possible further reform

This welter of criticism has led to calls for further reform. These tend to fall into a number of categories:

- A national primary.

- A series of four regional primaries: the Northeast, the South, the Midwest, the West.
- Further limits on money-raising and spending.
- A pre-primary mini-convention to choose the shortlist of candidates who would then run in the primaries.
- States voting in order of size of population, beginning with the smallest, followed by medium-sized states and finally the largest.

A plan based principally on the latter proposal was debated at the 2000 Republican National Convention but was defeated after George W. Bush let it be known he did not favour such a reform.

The are four problems with these reforms:
(1) The National Committees and Conventions of **both** parties would have to agree to the same reform.
(2) All 50 states would have to agree to change their state laws.
(3) A number of states strongly favour the current system over any of the proposals above.
(4) Limiting money-raising and spending would require an Act of Congress. Up until now there has been little agreement between the two parties on the subject of campaign finance reform.

3 National Party Conventions

3.1 The staging of National Party Conventions

Each of the major parties — and some minor parties — hold a National Party Convention. They are:
- held in the summer of the presidential election year (July/August/early September) and usually last for 4 days
- held in a large city: in 2008, Republicans in Minneapolis, Democrats in Denver
- held at a venue decided by each party's National Committee
- attended by delegates (most of them chosen in the primaries) and the media

3.2 The formal functions

These Conventions are said to have three **formal** functions:
(1) To choose the presidential candidate.
(2) To choose the vice-presidential candidate.
(3) To decide on the party platform (that is the policy document or 'manifesto').

3.2a Choosing the presidential candidate

This function has been lost almost entirely to the primaries. Almost all of the delegates who attend the Conventions are nowadays chosen in the primaries. They are chosen as 'committed delegates' — committed to voting for their candidate on the first ballot at the convention if he/she is still in the race.

To win the presidential nomination, a candidate must receive an absolute majority of the delegate votes. In 2008, there were 4,418 delegates attending the Democratic National Convention. Barack Obama therefore needed 2,210 votes to win the nomination. Once he had won that number of committed delegates — which he eventually achieved by early June — he was the certain nominee

This would certainly result in the primary season lasting longer than it does at present, because large-population states like California, New York and Texas would not vote until the end of the primary season.

Avoid the common error of candidates who state that the Conventions 'choose the president' and 'choose the vice-president'. They don't. They choose the presidential and vice-presidential *candidates*.

Don't worry too much about who the delegates are and exactly how they are chosen. Examiners will not expect that level of detail.

of his party, over 2 months before the Democratic National Convention met at the end of August.

It is therefore more accurate to state that the convention merely **confirms** rather than **chooses** the presidential candidate. Not since the Republican Convention of 1976 has the choice of the presidential candidate really been in any doubt at the opening of the convention. In that year, President Gerald Ford defeated ex-Governor Ronald Reagan by 1,187 delegate votes to 1,070.

3.2b Choosing the vice-presidential candidate

Again, this function has also been lost. Not since 1956 has a National Convention actually chosen the vice-presidential candidate or **running-mate**. Nowadays, the running-mate is chosen by the presidential candidate. Indeed, in recent years the announcement of the running-mate has been made *before* rather than *at* the National Convention. In 2008, both Barack Obama and John McCain announced their running-mates — Joe Biden and Sarah Palin, respectively — just before their Conventions convened. In 2004, John Kerry announced his choice of John Edwards 3 weeks before his party's National Convention.

It is therefore more accurate to state that the Convention merely **confirms** rather than **chooses** the vice-presidential candidate.

In choosing the vice-presidential candidate, the presidential candidate often looks for a **balanced ticket**. This means choosing a running-mate who is different from them in terms of:
- geographic region of origin or residence
- political experience
- age
- and maybe: gender, race, religion

A good example of a 'balanced ticket' would be the Democratic ticket in 1988 of Michael Dukakis and Lloyd Bentsen. This is shown in Table 2.6.

Characteristic	Michael Dukakis	Lloyd Bentsen
Political experience	State Governor	US Congress
Geographic region	Northeast (Massachusetts)	South (Texas)
Race and religion	Greek-American Greek Orthodox	White, Anglo-Saxon, Protestant (WASP)
Age	54	67
Ideology	liberal Democrat	conservative Democrat

Table 2.6 A balanced ticked: Dukakis–Bentsen, 1988

The party platform is what is called the 'manifesto' in British politics.

3.2c Deciding on the party platform

The party platform is the document containing the policies that the party intends to follow if it wins the election. The platform is put together by the **platform committee** under the direction of the party's national committee. The platform committee holds **hearings** around the country during the first 6 months of the election year. A draft platform is presented to delegates at the beginning of

These are known as 'floor fights'.

the convention. There may then be debates on various **planks** — parts of the platform. But nowadays, parties try to avoid heated and contentious debates at the convention. They feel it makes the party look divided — like the Republican Convention in 1992, in its disagreement over abortion.

3.3 The informal functions

The Conventions are said to have three *informal* functions:
● To promote party unity.
● To enthuse the party faithful.
● To enthuse the ordinary voters.

3.3a Promoting party unity

Promoting party unity is a very important function of the Conventions because:
● it is the only time in 4 years that the party actually meets together, during the rest of the time existing merely as 50 state parties
● any wounds created in the primaries can be healed
● it gives the defeated candidates an opportunity to support publicly the chosen candidate (e.g. Mitt Romney and Mike Huckabee supporting John McCain at the 2008 Republican Convention and Hillary Clinton supporting Barack Obama at the 2008 Democratic Convention)

The media will comment on whether or not the party is united. Disunited Conventions usually lead to defeat at the general election (e.g. Republicans 1992; Democrats 1980).

3.3b Enthusing the party faithful

Reference to the 'party faithful' means the delegates. It is important that they are 'enthused' by the candidates and the platform because:
● they are the people who will be organising and carrying out much of the campaigning at a state and local level
● they need to communicate that enthusiasm to ordinary voters in their own communities
● they therefore need to believe that they have a winning ticket and winning policies

3.3c Enthusing the ordinary voters

The 'ordinary voters' of course are not at the Convention. It is through television that the parties will hope to communicate with them, and especially through the media coverage of the presidential candidate's **acceptance speech** on the last night of the Convention. This is important because:
● it is the first opportunity for the presidential candidate to address ordinary voters
● the candidate will hope to display presidential qualities to voters
● the candidate will give an outline of the policies to be addressed
● the candidate will hope to boost their opinion poll ratings as a direct result — what is called **'bounce'** (see Table 2.7)

This was especially important for Governor George W. Bush in 2000 because typical American voters knew very little about him. He was the first Republican to win the presidential nomination of his party at the first attempt since Senator Barry Goldwater in 1964.

Year	Challenging party	Bounce	Incumbent party	Bounce
1968	Nixon (R)	+5	Humphrey (D)	+2
1972	McGovern (D)	0	Nixon (R)	+7
1976	Carter (D)	+9	Ford (R)	+5
1980	Reagan (R)	+8	Carter (D)	+10
1984	Mondale (D)	+9	Reagan (R)	+4
1988	Dukakis (D)	+7	Bush (R)	+6
1992	Clinton (D)	+16	Bush (R)	+5
1996	Dole (R)	+3	Clinton (D)	+5
2000	Bush (R)	+8	Gore (D)	+8
2004	Kerry (D)	+1	Bush (R)	+2
2008	Obama (D)	+4	McCain (R)	+6

Table 2.7 Post-Convention 'bounce', 1968–2008

Note Kerry's almost non-existent bounce in 2004.

3.4 The importance of modern-day Conventions

Many commentators suggest that, in comparison to Conventions of years ago, modern-day Conventions are of little importance because:
- the presidential candidates are chosen in the primaries
- the vice-presidential candidates are chosen by the presidential candidates and often announced before the Convention
- the parties try to lay on 'scripted' and 'sanitised' Conventions, devoid of controversy and hence of interest
- the terrestrial (as opposed to the cable) television companies have given less and less time to the coverage of Conventions

However, Conventions should not be too easily written off. Whilst the formal functions may have declined in importance, the informal functions are still very important. As presidential election scholar Stephen Wayne puts it, the Conventions 'may have become less newsworthy, but they are still important'.

4 *The general election campaign*

'intra' = within; 'inter' = between.

Labor Day is the US equivalent of the August Bank Holiday in the UK.

The general election:
- is when the **intra-party** campaign has finished and the **inter-party** campaign begins
- by tradition begins on Labor Day — the first Monday in September — but recently has begun straight after the Conventions
- runs for 8–9 weeks until the day before election day in early November
- is very expensive
- is conducted largely on television
- includes the televised presidential debates — usually three of them during October — plus one televised debate between the two vice-presidential candidates (see Topic 2.6.3b)

The candidates will tour the country, spending time in states that have large numbers of Electoral College votes and/or which are seen as 'swing' states, that is, could be won by either party.

5 Campaign finance

5.1 Pre-reforms

US election campaigns are often criticised for spending vast sums of money. Such criticism may well have merit, but it is important to remember some of the reasons why US elections are so expensive, especially when compared with UK parliamentary elections:

- The country is vast (the entire UK is the size of Oregon).
- The elections are not just to elect one legislative chamber (as in the UK).
- The general election campaign lasts 9 weeks, not 3–4 weeks as in the UK.
- Candidates must contest the primaries, which begin 9 months before election day.
- There is no 'free time' on US television; buying time is expensive.

Until the 1970s, campaign finance was largely unregulated, which meant that:

- personal wealth was important in running for political office (e.g. JFK in 1960)
- people were not limited in the sums they could give to candidates
- **'fat cats'** gave huge sums (often running into millions of dollars) to candidates
- candidates were not limited in the sums they could spend on their campaigns
- many opportunities for corruption existed

> Be careful when writing about the importance of money. It is misleading to say that someone 'needs a lot of money' to run for the presidency. That could be taken to mean that you have to be personally wealthy. Say, rather, that someone 'needs to raise a lot of money' to run for the presidency.

5.2 The 1970s reforms

A number of events occurred in the 1970s that led to a different system of campaign finance:

- Congress began to pass legislation in 1971 to restrict campaign contributions and expenditure.
- The Watergate affair acted as a catalyst for change.
- Congress passed another campaign finance law in 1974.

The Federal Election Campaign Act (1974):

- limited individual contributions to a candidate to $1,000
- limited corporate contributions to a candidate to $5,000
- forbade donations from foreign donors
- limited candidates' expenditure to $10 million (1974) in the primaries and a further $20 million (1974) in the general election — these figures to be index-linked for inflation every 4 years
- provided for **'matching funds'** from the federal tax payer to help finance presidential elections
- established the **Federal Election Commission** (FEC) to enforce and regulate this new system

> Don't confuse this with the 'matching funds' given by the federal government to states to help them provide certain services.

5.3 The 2002 reforms

But the 1970s reforms left a number of loopholes which became new and significant problems during the elections of the 1980s and 1990s. These included problems concerning:

- 'soft money' spent by political parties on 'party building' or 'get-out-the-vote' activities
- the growth in 'issue advocacy' campaigning by, for example, abortion, environmental and labour union groups
- the weakening of the political parties as 'matching funds' went directly to the candidates' organisations rather than to the parties
- the failure of the Federal Election Commission to have much in the way of enforcement powers against those who broke the new rules

Following the campaign finance abuses surrounding Bill Clinton's re-election campaign, Republican Senator John McCain made campaign finance reform a key issue in his (eventually unsuccessful) campaign for the Republican presidential nomination in 2000. But eventually, along with Democrat Senator Russell Feingold, he was successful in getting another raft of reforms passed through Congress in 2002.

The principal changes brought about by the 2002 reforms were:
- National Party Committees banned from raising or spending 'soft money'
- labour unions and corporate groups forbidden from directly funding issue advertisements
- the banning of union or corporate money to fund advertisements that mention a federal candidate, within 60 days of a general election or 30 days of a primary
- the prohibition of fundraising on federal property
- increased individual limits on contributions to individual candidates or candidate committees to $2,300 (2007–08), to be increased for inflation in each odd-numbered year
- banned contributions from foreign nationals
- 'Stand By Your Ad' provision, resulting in all campaign ads including a verbal endorsement by the candidate with the words: 'I'm [candidate's name] and I approve this message'

6 *The media*

The term 'the media' includes print journalism, radio and television, though the latter is the most important in this context.

6.1 Newspapers

There are no national titles, except for *USA Today* (a weekday broadsheet) and the *Wall Street Journal* (the US equivalent of the UK's *Financial Times*). But there are local papers that have a national reputation, such as the *Washington Post* and the *New York Times*. What is most important is what these kinds of papers say on their 'op–ed' (short for 'opinion–editorial') pages as well as the endorsements they make of particular candidates near to election day. Don't forget also the websites that these and other newspapers now maintain.

For example: www.
washingtonpost.com
and www.nytimes.com

6.2 Journals

These are weeklies aimed at a general readership. The main titles are *Time* and *Newsweek*, but *US News and World Report* is in the same market, though aimed at a more specifically political audience. 'Cover stories' are the most important factor of these journals; that is, the inside story which features on the cover of that week's edition. Again, related websites are now used extensively.

6.3 Television

6.3a Different types and forms of television

Television is the principal medium for imparting information during a US election. It exists in two forms:

(1) terrestrial — the 'networks': ABC, CBS, NBC and PBS
(2) cable: CNN, Fox News, MSNBC, C-SPAN.

Television carries mainly three different forms of political information and coverage:

(1) **Daily news programmes:** e.g. ABC's *Good Morning America* and *World News Tonight.*
(2) **Nightly/weekly documentary programmes:** e.g. *The News Hour with Jim Lehrer* (PBS), *Inside Politics* (CNN), *The McLaughlin Group* (NBC), which will contain serious political interviews.
(3) **Chat shows:** e.g. *Larry King Live* (CNN).
(4) **Comedy shows:** e.g. *Saturday Night Live* (NBC).

6.3b The televised presidential debates

There are now the traditional televised presidential debates during the general election campaign. These began in 1960, between Kennedy and Nixon, but were not used again until 1976, between Ford and Carter. They have been used in every election year since then. There are usually three presidential and one vice-presidential debate, each lasting 1½ hours. They generally include only Democrat and Republican candidates, though Ross Perot and his running-mate James Stockdale were included in 1992. Most have been in the format of a joint press conference with a panel of journalists asking questions. But from 1992, 'town hall' style debates have also been used — a more informal style with questions put by an invited audience. The 2000 debates saw another new format — the round-table discussion, in which candidates talk with each other rather than *at* each other or *to* an audience.

These debates can be important. The following rules of thumb should be noted:

(1) Style is often more important than substance — it's not what you say, but how you say it and how you look.
(2) Avoid serious gaffes.
(3) Look for opportunities to deliver a 'sound bite' that will be used by the news organisations in their 'highlights'.
(4) Debates are more difficult for incumbent presidents than for challengers because incumbents have a record to defend and can have their words from 4 years ago quoted back at them.

6.3c Television commercials

Television commercials date from the 1952 campaign. They are usually 30-second commercials, but may be longer nearer election day.

Also good websites — for example www.abcnews.com, www.cnn.com

In this sense they are not really 'debates' at all, as there is no communication between the candidates.

For example, Bush having to defend breaking his 1988 'No New Taxes' pledge in the 1992 debates with Clinton.

There are different types of commercials. There are those that are **positive** about your candidate. These may be either **biographical** or **policy-orientated**. There are also **negative** commercials, talking only about your opponent. These may be either **'attack ads'** or **humorous** — attempting to poke fun at your opponent.

Discussion regarding television commercials centres upon:
- cost
- whether 'attack ads' are double-edged swords, which hurt the purveyor more than the intended target
- the extent to which commercials change voters' minds and voting intentions
- evidence that commercials do little in the way of **'conversion'** but more in terms of **'reinforcement'** and **'activation'** — reinforcing what voters already think and activating them to turn out and vote for your candidate

7 *Election day and the Electoral College*

7.1 Election day

On election day:
- all registered voters are eligible to vote
- only around 50% of registered voters will vote
- polling stations are open at times decided by state law — usually from 7 or 8 a.m. to 7 or 8 p.m.
- once the polls close, votes are counted in each state
- the television networks will announce results based mostly on exit polls
- the television networks 'award' the Electoral College votes of each state on a winner-takes-all basis and announce the overall winner usually about 4–5 hours after the polls close on the east coast

7.2 The Electoral College

7.2a How it works

Each state is awarded a certain number of Electoral College votes (ECVs). This number is equal to that state's representation in Congress — the number of Senators (2) plus the number of Representatives. Thus in 2008, California had 55 ECVs whilst Wyoming had only three.

There are a total of 538 ECVs. To win the presidency, a candidate must win an **absolute majority** of ECVs — that is 270.

The popular votes are counted in each state. Whichever candidate wins the most popular votes in a state receives all the ECVs of that state. This is not in the Constitution, but 48 of the 50 states have a state law requiring it. The other two states — Maine and Nebraska — award ECVs on a different basis, depending on who wins the presidential vote in each congressional district.

The Electoral College never meets together. The Electors meet in their respective state capitals on the Monday after the second Wednesday in December and send their results to the vice-president in Washington DC.

It is the *number* equal to the state's representation in Congress, not the Senate and House *members* themselves.

Be careful to get this right. An absolute majority is more than everyone else put together: 50% + 1.

Don't worry too much about who the Electors actually are. Examiners will not expect you to know that level of detail.

Year	Candidates	Popular vote (%)	Electoral College vote
1968	**Richard Nixon/Spiro Agnew (R)**	43.2	301
	Hubert Humphrey/Edmund Muskie (D)	42.7	191
	George Wallace/Curtis LeMay (I)	13.5	46
1972	**Richard Nixon/Spiro Agnew (R)**	60.7	520
	George McGovern/Sargent Shriver (D)	37.5	17
1976	**Jimmy Carter/Walter Mondale (D)**	50.1	297
	Gerald Ford/Bob Dole (R)	48.0	240
1980	**Ronald Reagan/George H.W. Bush (R)**	50.7	489
	Jimmy Carter/Walter Mondale (D)	41.0	49
1984	**Ronald Reagan/George H.W. Bush (R)**	58.8	525
	Walter Mondale/Geraldine Ferraro (D)	40.6	13
1988	**George H.W. Bush/Dan Quayle (R)**	53.4	426
	Michael Dukakis/Lloyd Bentsen (D)	45.6	111
1992	**Bill Clinton/Al Gore (D)**	43.0	370
	George H.W. Bush/Dan Quayle (R)	37.5	168
	Ross Perot/James Stockdale (I)	18.9	0
1996	**Bill Clinton/Al Gore (D)**	49.2	379
	Bob Dole/Jack Kemp (R)	40.7	159
2000	**George W. Bush/Dick Cheney (R)**	47.9	271
	Al Gore/Joe Lieberman (D)	48.4	266
2004	**George W. Bush/Dick Cheney (R)**	50.7	286
	John Kerry/John Edwards (D)	48.3	252
2008	**Barack Obama/Joe Biden (D)**	52.7	365
	John McCain/Sarah Palin (R)	45.7	173

Table 2.8 Presidential election results, 1968–2008 (winners in bold)

The vice-president announces the result to a joint session of Congress in early January. If no candidate wins 270 ECVs, the president will be elected by the House of Representatives, with each *state* having one vote — that is a total of 50 votes. The winner would have to receive an absolute majority (26) of those votes. Balloting would continue until this occurred. Meanwhile, the vice-president would be elected by the Senate with each senator having one vote — that is a total of 100 votes. The winner would need to receive an absolute majority (51) of those votes. Balloting would continue until this occurred. Only twice has the Electoral College failed to come up with a winner and the election been thrown to Congress — 1800 and 1824.

7.2b The strengths of the Electoral College system
There are two principal strengths of the Electoral College system:
(1) It preserves the voice of the small-population states.
(2) It promotes a two-horse race, with the winner therefore receiving over 50% of the popular vote, giving the president a mandate to govern. In 25 of the last 37 elections (67%), the winner gained more than 50% of the popular vote.

7.2c The weaknesses of the Electoral College system
However, there are a number of weaknesses associated with the Electoral College system. Amongst them are the following:

However, three of the 12 in which the winner has not received at least 50% of the popular vote were 1992, 1996 and 2000 (see Table 2.8).

(1) Small states are over-represented. This is because every state, regardless of population, has two senators and one House member. Wyoming has three ECVs for its roughly half-a-million people. California has 55 ECVs for its over 30 million. Thus, although California has over 60 times as many people, it gets only 18 times as many ECVs as Wyoming. If California had ECVs on the same basis as Wyoming, it should have 180 of them!

Not the case in 2004.

(2) The winner-takes-all system can distort the result. In 2008, Obama won just over 52% of the popular vote but 68% of the ECVs.

(3) It is possible for a candidate to win the overall popular vote throughout the 50 states but lose in the Electoral College. This occurred in 2000, when Gore polled just under 540,000 more votes nationwide than Bush but lost 271–266 in the Electoral College. This has occurred twice before, in 1876 and 1888, and almost occurred in 1960 and 1968 (see Table 2.9).

It should have been 271–267 but one Elector from Washington DC refused to cast her vote for Al Gore in protest against the city's lack of represen-tation in Congress.

Year	Candidates	Popular vote (%)	Electoral College vote
1876	Samuel Tilden (D)	51.0	184
	Rutherford Hayes (R)	47.9	185
1888	Grover Cleveland (D)	48.6	168
	Benjamin Harrison (R)	47.8	233
1960	**John Kennedy (D)**	49.8	303
	Richard Nixon (R)	49.5	219
1968	**Richard Nixon (R)**	43.2	301
	Hubert Humphrey (D)	42.7	191
	George Wallace (I)	13.5	46
2000	Al Gore (D)	48.4	266
	George W. Bush (R)	47.9	271

Table 2.9 Presidential elections: selected results (winners in bold)

It is important to say 'national' third parties, as 'regional' third parties — such as George Wallace's Independent Party in 1968 — can win Electoral College votes more easily.

(4) It is very unfair to **national** third parties. In 1992, Ross Perot gained 19% of the popular vote but won no ECVs.

Year	State	Number of Electors	Elector should have voted for	Elector actually voted for
1960	Alabama	6	John Kennedy	Harry Byrd
	Mississippi	8	John Kennedy	Harry Byrd
	Oklahoma	1	Richard Nixon	Harry Byrd
1968	North Carolina	1	Richard Nixon	George Wallace
1972	Virginia	1	Richard Nixon	John Hospers
1976	Washington	1	Gerald Ford	Ronald Reagan
1988	West Virginia	1	Michael Dukakis	Lloyd Bentsen
2000	Washington DC	1	Al Gore	No-one
2004	Minnesota	1	John Kerry	John Edwards

Table 2.10 'Rogue Electors', 1960–2004

(5) So-called 'rogue' or 'faithless' Electors vote for candidates other than the one who won the popular vote in their state (see Table 2.10).

(6) The system used in the case of an Electoral College deadlock could result in the House choosing a president of one party and the Senate choosing a vice-president of another party.

7.2d Possible reforms of the Electoral College system

Here are three possible reforms of the Electoral College system:

(1) Abandon the winner-takes-all system for **a more proportional system** (already used by two states — Maine and Nebraska). Had Florida been using a proportional system in 2000, it might have eased the problem. Instead of deciding who was going to get 25 ECVs and who was going to get none, it might have instead decided who got 13 ECVs and who got 12.

(2) Pass state laws to **prohibit 'rogue' Electors** from casting such rogue votes.

(3) **Abolish the Electoral College altogether** and decide the election on the popular vote. The problem with this is it would encourage a multi-candidate election with the winner gaining maybe only 35–40% of the votes.

> But remember: all reforms require either changes in state laws or a constitutional amendment. Both are very difficult to achieve and therefore unlikely.

8 | *Voting behaviour in presidential elections*

The subject of voting behaviour attempts to answer these kinds of questions about why people vote as they do:

- How important is party affiliation?
- Are there differences in the voting habits of men and women?
- How important is race in voting?
- What about religious groups?
- What about the voting habits of the poor as opposed to the better-off?
- Does geographic region have anything to tell us?
- What role do policies play?

8.1 Party affiliation

Despite all we say about political parties not being all that important in US politics, party affiliation seems to be an important ingredient in determining voting. In the 2008 presidential election:

- 71% of voters identified with one of the two major parties: 39% called themselves Democrats; 32% called themselves Republicans
- 89% of the Democrats voted for Obama
- 90% of the Republicans voted for McCain

In the presidential elections between 1952 and 2008, the party that managed to gain the highest level of support from its own identifiers won on 12 out of 15 occasions, but 2008 was one of the three occasions when this was not the case.

Winning elections is as much about **mobilising** your own supporters as it is about **converting** supporters of your opponent so that they vote for you. It is also about who manages to get people to the voting booths on election day. Do your supporters turn out or stay at home? Elections are determined just as much by the stay-at-homes as by those who turn up to vote.

8.2 Gender

With regards to gender and voting, the following points are worth noting:

- Women are more likely to be registered voters than men.
- Women tend to turn out in higher numbers on election day than men.
- In recent elections, the trend has been for men to be more supportive of Republican candidates whilst women have tended to support the Democrats. (But in 2008, men split 49-48 for Obama.)
- In the presidential elections between 1964 and 2008, women were more supportive than men of the Democrats in 11 out of 12 elections. (In 2008, women voted 56-43 for Obama.)
- Women are more likely to be registered Democrats than registered Republicans.

The reasons for this are thought to derive from the stance of the two major parties on such policies as:

- **abortion** — Democrats tend to be pro-choice and Republicans tend to be pro-life
- **defence** — women tend to favour lower levels of spending; the Democrats' position
- **law and order** — women tend to oppose capital punishment; again the Democrats' position
- **gun control** — women tend to support this; another Democrat position
- **women's rights** — Democrats supported the Equal Rights Amendment; Republicans tended to oppose it.

So, to win elections, the Republicans are always looking for ways to appeal more to women voters, whilst Democrats are trying to attract more male voters. And because there are more women than men amongst registered voters, the larger the turnout, the better it is for the Democrats.

8.3 Race

8.3a African-Americans

African-Americans, who make up some 10% of the US electorate, have since the 1960s given solid support to the Democratic Party. Traditionally, the Republicans — 'the party of Lincoln' — had thought of the black vote as theirs, following Lincoln's freeing of the slaves after the Civil War. But that changed during the twentieth century for two reasons. First, it was Democrat Franklin Roosevelt's 'New Deal' that helped out-of-work and poor African-Americans in the 1930s. Second, Democrats Kennedy and Johnson got Congress to pass civil rights laws that protected the rights of African-Americans in such matters as housing, education, employment and voting. In the eight presidential elections between 1980 and 2008, African-Americans never gave less than 83% support to the Democrat candidate. In 2008, it was 95%.

8.3b Hispanics

Hispanics are a more diverse group and encompass:

- Cuban-Americans
- Mexican-Americans
- Puerto Rican-Americans
- those from other Central American countries

But they are a numerically growing group. Hence their importance increases at each election.

Category	% of electorate	Obama (%)	McCain (%)
All	100	53	46
Democrats	39	89	10
Republicans	32	9	90
Independents	29	52	44
Men	47	49	48
Women	53	56	43
White men	36	41	57
White women	39	46	53
Black men	5	95	5
Black women	7	96	3
Protestant	54	45	54
Catholic	27	54	45
Jewish	2	78	21
Family income:			
Under $15,000	6	73	25
$15,000–$29,999	12	60	37
$30,000–$49,999	19	55	43
$50,000–$74,999	21	48	49
$75,000–$99,999	15	51	48
$100,000–$149,999	14	48	51
$150,000–$199,999	6	48	50
Over $200,000	6	52	46
East	21	59	40
Midwest	24	54	44
South	32	45	54
West	22	57	40

Table 2.11 Who voted for whom, 2008

Cuban-Americans, especially those in South Florida, have tended to support Republican candidates. Other Hispanic groups, such as those in California and New Mexico, have tended to support Democrats.

In the 2000 and 2004 elections, the Republicans were seen courting the Hispanic vote. In 1992, George H.W. Bush won just 24% of the Hispanic vote. In 1996, it dropped to 20% for Bob Dole. By 2004 it was 43% for George W. Bush, but this fell back to just 31% for John McCain in 2008.

8.4 Religion

There are certain trends in voting according to religion, a factor much stronger in US politics than in the UK. Note the following four points:

(1) **Protestant voters tend to vote Republican.** They didn't give Clinton a majority of their votes in either 1992 or 1996 — they went for George H.W. Bush in 1992 (45%–34%) and for Dole in 1996 (47%–43%). In 2004, they broke in favour of George W. Bush (59%–40%) and in favour of McCain (54%–45%) in 2008.

(2) **Catholic voters tend to vote Democrat**, though not as strongly as used to be the case. But they did give Clinton a 54%–37% vote in 1992 and 42%–37% in 1996. The Democrats' pro-choice position on abortion can be a liability with Catholic voters. But in 2004, Bush won the majority of Catholic voters — 52%–47%. In 2008, Obama won 54% of Catholic voters with just 45% going for McCain.

(3) **Jewish voters tend to vote Democrat** pretty solidly. (But they make up only 3% of the electorate.) They gave Clinton 78% support in both 1992 and 1996. They have given a majority of their votes to the Democrat candidate in every presidential election since the Second World War. In 2000, they gave 79% support to the Gore–Lieberman ticket. So Al Gore's choice of Joseph Lieberman — an orthodox Jew — as his running-mate in 2000 did not obviously help him politically with Jews.

(4) In the 2000 presidential election, there was a **high correlation between attendance at religious services and voting Republican**. Of those voters who attend religious services weekly or more than weekly — and that was 42% of all voters — 63% voted for George W. Bush, but this correlation was much less clear in 2008.

The figure in the UK is 8%!

8.5 Wealth

There is a strong correlation between relative wealth and likely support of the two major parties. In both 1992 and 1996, Clinton had his highest support amongst those earning under $15,000 (£10,000) a year and his lowest support amongst those earning over $100,00 (£66,000) a year. Likewise, in both elections, the Republicans received their lowest support among the poorest and their highest support among the most wealthy. The pattern was repeated in 2004, with Kerry winning 63% of the poorest voters but only 41% of the wealthiest, whilst Bush won only 36% of the poorest voters but 58% of the wealthiest. In 2008, Obama won a majority amongst both the very poor (73%) and the very rich (52%).

8.6 Geographic region

There are certain trends in voting according to geographic region. Consider the following four points:

For example Boston, New York, Philadelphia, Baltimore.

(1) **The Northeast tends to support the Democrats.** The region's big cities gave Bill Clinton his highest level of support in any region in both 1992 and 1996 and likewise for Gore in 2000, Kerry in 2004 and Obama in 2008. Bad news for the Democrats — demographically, the Northeast is a declining region. Fewer people means less political clout.

(2) From the end of the Civil War in the 1860s until the 1960s, the South was described as 'the solid South' — voting solidly for the Democratic Party. The rule was simply 'vote as you shot'. But in the last three decades of the twentieth century, **the 'solid South' for the Democrats has collapsed**. The South voted for George H.W. Bush in 1992, Bob Dole in 1996, for George W. Bush in 2000 and 2004, and for John McCain in 2008. In 2008, the South was the only region to vote Republican. But strength in the South is good news for the Republicans — demographically the South is a growing region. More people means more political clout.

(3) **The West tends to support the Democrats**. States such as California, Oregon and Washington voted solidly for Clinton in 1992 and 1996, although Green Party candidate Ralph Nader nibbled away at Gore's majority in the Pacific Northwest in 2000. Kerry won all three west coast states in 2004, as did Obama in 2008.

(4) **The Midwest is the battle-ground in modern elections.** In 2000, the Midwest broke 49%–48% between Bush and Gore. Nationally it was 48%–48%. In 2004, the Midwest broke 51%–48% between Bush and Kerry, exactly the same as the national vote. And in 2008, Obama won the Midwest 54%–44%, very similar to the national vote. Today's presidential elections are largely won and lost in Missouri, Michigan and Ohio. Between 1960 and 2004, whoever won Missouri won the White House — true for all 12 presidential elections, but not in 2008, with McCain winning the state by just one percentage point. But Obama did win Michigan and Ohio. Ohio has now voted for the winner in every presidential election since 1964.

8.7 Policies

Policies matter, but which ones? They can easily change from one election to another. Here are five important points to note about policies and voting:

(1) In the **1992** election, it was 'the economy, stupid!' In that election, voters who thought the economy was in 'good shape' voted 82% for George H.W. Bush, whilst those who thought it in 'poor shape' voted 65% for Bill Clinton. The trouble for Bush was that twice as many voters fell into the second category as into the first.

(2) In **1992**, Bush also suffered from the fact that in an election in which he was trumpeting his foreign policy successes — most notably, victory in the Persian Gulf War — only 8% of voters thought that foreign policy mattered as an issue. That figure had been 23% back in 1988 when Bush was elected.

(3) In **2000**, the four issues most frequently mentioned by voters as being those that mattered were: the economy and jobs; education; social security; taxes. But voters preferred Al Gore's position on the first three. Only on taxes did George W. Bush have a majority who preferred his policies — but it was 80%–17%!

(4) In **2004**, the four main issues were 'moral values', the economy/jobs, terrorism and Iraq. When 2004 voters were asked which issue mattered most in deciding their vote, 22% said 'moral values', 20% said the economy and jobs, 19% said terrorism and 15% the war in Iraq.

(5) In **2008**, 63% of voters in exit polls said that the economy was the most important issue, with the second most important issue — the war in Iraq — being named by only 10% of voters (see Table 2.12). Amongst the 63% of voters who identified the economy as the most important issue, Obama beat McCain by 53% to 44%, almost the same as the nationwide popular vote.

Which issues mattered most in deciding your vote?	% of electorate	Obama (%)	McCain (%)
The economy	63	53	44
The war in Iraq	10	59	39
Terrorism	9	13	86
Health care	9	73	26
Energy policy	7	50	46

Table 2.12 Issues and voting, 2008

8.8 Typical voters

- The old Democrat **'New Deal coalition'** has weakened.
- During the 1990s, Bill Clinton tried to move the Democratic Party away from its old 'tax and spend', liberal base to a more centrist 'third way'.
- The Democrats have lost significant support amongst Southern whites and have a problem attracting male voters, but they are still very strong in the Northeast.
- The Republicans have experienced difficulties attracting women voters and those of racial minorities but they are very strong amongst white, evangelical Christians and in the so-called 'sun-belt' states.
- Typical Democrat voting blocs: blue-collar, unionised workers; urban dwellers; West and Northeast; Catholic; Jewish; racial minority, possibly black or Hispanic; female; liberal; less wealthy; less well-educated.
- Typical Republican voting blocs: white-collar, professional workers; suburban and rural; sun-belt; Protestant, especially evangelical; white; male; conservative; wealthy; college-educated.

This refers to a coalition including urban workers, racial minorities, farmers, southerners and liberals.

B Congressional elections

1 An overview

Congressional elections:
- are elections for the House of Representatives and the Senate
- occur every 2 years when the whole of the House of Representatives and one-third of the Senate are elected
- coincide either with the presidential election (in years divisible by 4, i.e.2004, 2008, 2012 etc.) or occur midway through the presidential term (called **'mid-term elections'** — in 2006, 2010, 2014 etc.)

A district, or in full, a congressional district, is the US equivalent of the UK term 'constituency' and is the geographic area represented by a member of the House of Representatives.

Especially large-geographic, large-population states such as California and New York.

The Constitution (Article I) states that to be eligible to be a member of Congress, one must fulfil certain requirements regarding age, citizenship and residency. To be a member of the House of Representatives, one must:

- be at least 25 years of age
- have been a US citizen for at least 7 years
- be a resident of the state your district is in

Some states have a **locality rule** which means that House members must be resident of the district they represent.

To be a member of the Senate, one must:

- be at least 30 years of age
- have been a US citizen for at least 9 years
- be a resident of the state you represent

2 Primaries

To avoid confusion, I prefer to use the term 'House members' to refer to members of the House of Representatives.

Candidates for congressional elections must first secure the nomination of their party. As virtually all 535 members of Congress are either Democrats or Republicans, this means securing the nomination of one of the two major parties through the Democratic or Republican congressional primary. Sometimes, even an incumbent House member or senator might be challenged for the nomination in the upcoming election and will therefore have to enter the primary. Defeat for incumbents in the primary is highly unusual. Between 1982 and 2008 — 14 election cycles — only 62 House members and a mere four senators were defeated in congressional primaries.

3 Trends in congressional elections

3.1 Coat-tails effect

The **coat-tails effect** is the effect of a strong candidate for a party at the top of the ticket (i.e. president, state governor) helping congressional candidates of the same party to get elected at the same time. The coat-tails effect had not been evident in elections for over two decades. In 1980, the Republican presidential candidate Ronald Reagan helped the Republicans gain 33 seats in the House and 12 seats in the Senate. But in 2008, Democrat presidential candidate Barack Obama helped the Democrats gain 21 seats in the House and eight seats in the Senate, leading some commentators to say that Obama was the first president since Reagan to have genuine coat-tails.

3.2 Split-ticket voting

Split-ticket voting is the practice of voting for candidates of two or more parties for different offices at the same election. The opposite — voting for candidates of the same party for different offices at the same election — is called **straight-ticket voting**. In 2008, just 83 congressional districts (19% of the total) voted differently in the presidential and House elections. In 34 districts, Obama won the presidential race but the Republican won the House race; 49 districts voted McCain for president but Democrat in the House race.

Split-ticket voting in congressional elections which coincide with the presidential election may result in **divided government** — one party controlling the White House, whilst the other party controls the two houses of Congress. This occurred in 1996, when voters re-elected Democrat president Bill Clinton but also elected Republican majorities to both the House and the Senate. In the 40 years between 1969 and 2009, the US had divided government for 22 years, including the last 6 years of Bill Clinton's presidency (1995–2001) and the last 2 years of George W. Bush's presidency (2007–09).

3.3 The power of incumbency

An **incumbent** is the House member or senator who currently holds the seat. Congressional elections show very high levels of support for incumbents, or put another way, there are very high rates of re-election in congressional elections. In the House, re-election rates have exceeded 95% in six of the last 11 congressional elections, though 2006 and 2008 were two elections when this did not occur. In the same period (1988–2008), re-election rates in the Senate ranged from a high of 96% in 2004 to a low of 79% in 2006.

3.4 Decline in competitive races in House elections

Between 1992 and 2004, there was a significant trend towards fewer genuinely competitive seats in elections to the House of Representatives. A competitive seat is one that was won by the incumbent by less than 10 percentage points. In 1992, there were 111 such seats in the House. By 2004, the figure had fallen to just 31. In other words, following the 2004 congressional elections, 404 out of the 435 House members — or just under 93% — were in what we would call safe seats. Both the 2006 and 2008 congressional elections saw increases in the numbers of competitive House races.

There are two important consequences when House seats become uncompetitive. First, incumbents in safe seats tend to vote in the House in a way which pleases only those voters from their own party. This leads to an increase in **partisanship** and a decrease in compromise and cross-party cooperation. Second, House members in safe seats have more to fear from an intra-party challenge in a primary than from an inter-party challenge in the general election. Hence the primary becomes the real political battleground and winning the primary is tantamount to winning re-election.

3.5 The White House party tends to lose seats in mid-term elections

The mid-term elections are those which occur midway through a president's term, such as those held in 2002, 2006 or 2010. In the 92-year period since the Senate was first directly elected (1914–2006), the president's party has lost an average of 29 seats in the House and four seats in the Senate in mid-term elections. In 1994, for example, President Clinton's Democratic Party lost 52 House seats and eight Senate seats. In 2006, President Bush's Republican Party lost 30 House seats and six Senate seats. During this 92-year period, on only two occasions — 1934 and 2002 — has the president's party gained seats in both houses in the mid-term elections. In 2002, Bush's Republicans gained five House seats and two Senate seats.

Largely as a result of the events of 11 September 2001 (9/11) and Bush's 'war on terror'.

Questions

18 Explain the term 'divided government'.

19 Explain the term 'incumbent'.

20 Explain each of the following terms: **(a)** proposition or initiative; **(b)** referendum; **(c)** recall election.

Political parties are, of course, important in any democracy. But in the USA they are less important than in many other democracies — such as the UK, for example. First, the USA is so vast that organising a political party across the length and breadth of the country is rather different from organising a party in the UK. In the USA, as we shall see, parties are more state-based than national. Second, elections in the USA have become much more candidate-centred affairs than they tend to be in the UK, where voters still have quite strong national party ties. In the UK, many people will vote 'Labour' or 'Conservative'. In the USA, people will tend to vote 'Obama' or 'McCain' — or whoever.

The topic is divided into three major headings:

A Party organisation, philosophy, ideology and partisanship

B The two-party system

C Third parties

A Party organisation, philosophy, ideology and partisanship

1 *National organisation*

The USA has a federal system of government (see Topic 1.E). Federalism is a decentralised form of government. Some powers are vested in the national government, but other equally important powers are vested in the state governments. The more centralised the government, the more centralised the party system. The less centralised the government, the less centralised the party system. Thus, US political parties are **decentralised**. Certainly there is some national organisation, but it does not amount to very much. US political parties are principally state-based.

In the USA, the Republican Party is often referred to as the GOP — 'The Grand Old Party'.

The two major US parties — the Democrats and the Republicans — do have something of a national party organisation, but it is fairly limited. Each has a National Committee. The Democratic National Committee (DNC) and the Republican National Committee (RNC) are each headed by a party chairperson. He or she acts as a spokesperson for the national party, especially in the media, and is responsible for the day-to-day running of the party. Although the DNC and RNC meet in full session only twice a year, they are permanent organisations with offices in Washington DC. And, of course, each party holds a National Convention once every 4 years (see Topic 2.A.3). But that is about it.

2 State organisation

Everything else is done at the state or local level. At that level, the organisation of each party looks something like this:

- State Party Convention
- State Party Committee (headed by State Party Chairperson)
- County Committees
- District Committees
- City Committees
- Ward Committees
- Precinct Committees

In essays, make a comparison with the very different situation in UK parties.

So it is worth noting that US political parties really have no one who can truly be called the 'party leader'. The president might be said to be 'the leader' of the party. But even that does not mean very much. The party not in control of the White House does not even have that level of national leadership. Except for the period — once every 4 years — between the National Party Convention and the holding of the presidential election, when both parties do have someone who maybe looks and sounds like a national leader, US national political parties are pretty leaderless.

3 Philosophy and ideology

In terms of philosophy and ideology, both major parties in the USA are quite diverse. The Democratic Party is usually associated with being the more liberal of the two. Yet Democrats come in many shades — 'liberal Democrats', 'moderate Democrats', 'New Democrats' and even 'conservative Democrats'.

It is important to use correctly the words 'conservative' (i.e. the adjective) and 'Conservative' (i.e. the name of a party).

The Republican Party is normally thought of as being the more conservative of the two parties. Yet there are 'moderate Republicans', 'conservative Republicans', 'Christian conservatives' and, more recently, 'compassionate conservatives'. ('Compassionate conservative' was popularised as a term by George W. Bush in the 2000 election.)

In the 1960s, the Democratic Party contained both 'liberal Democrats' (like President John Kennedy and his brothers senators Robert and Edward Kennedy, pushing for civil rights for African-Americans) and 'conservative Democrats' (like Governor George Wallace of Alabama, whom many would have regarded as an unreformed racist).

Even today, the Republican Party contains a huge spectrum of opinion, from a 'conservative Republican' like Senator John Kyl of Arizona to a 'moderate Republican' like Senator Olympia Snowe of Maine. Meanwhile, the Democratic Party contains 'liberals' like Senator Barbara Boxer of California on the one hand and 'conservatives' like Senator Blanche Lincoln of Arkansas on the other.

The key to understanding much of this is geography. In the Northeast — in states like New York, Massachusetts or Maine — one will tend to find 'liberal

Democrats' and 'moderate Republicans'. The same is true on the west coast — in states such as California or Oregon. But in the South — in states like Louisiana, Alabama, North and South Carolina — you will tend to come across 'conservative Democrats' and 'conservative Republicans'. Both parties take on different ideological colours from region to region. If they didn't, they wouldn't be national parties. And if they weren't national parties, they wouldn't win the presidency — the greatest prize of US politics.

There was a time was when the southern states were referred to as the **'solid South'**. This was because voters in the South voted solidly for the Democratic Party. This was a consequence of the Civil War, fought in the 1860s. During the Civil War, the Republicans were thought of as the party of the North, the Democrats as the party of the South. And for a century and more later, people in the South would use the slogan **'vote as you shot'**. It wasn't until quite recently, as is shown in Table 3.1, that the South became part of the competitive two-party system.

4 *Partisanship*

With the final collapse of the 'solid South' in the 1990s, both parties became more ideologically cohesive. Southern conservative Democrats transferred to the Republican Party leaving the Democrats a more cohesively liberal party. And the absorbing of southern conservatives into the Republican Party made that party even more conservative. As US politics moved into the twenty-first century, pundits started to talk about the USA as a **'50–50 nation'**, split in half between **red America** (voting Republican) and **blue America** (voting Democrat). This was most plainly seen in the 2000 elections in which both parties ended up with around 49% of the popular vote, the Electoral College vote split 271–267, the House of Representatives was 221–212 with two independents, while the Senate split exactly 50–50.

Red America was portrayed as:
- more male than female
- overwhelmingly white
- Protestant and, specifically, born-again evangelical
- wealthy
- rural (and maybe suburban)
- Southern or Midwestern
- conservative

Blue America, in contrast, was portrayed as:
- more female than male
- a rainbow coalition of white, black, Hispanic and Asian
- Catholic, but not especially church-going
- less wealthy
- predominantly urban
- North-eastern, Great Lakes or west coast
- liberal

Commentators also noticed increased partisanship in US politics — be it in voting behaviour amongst the electorate, or the tone of debate and voting

Red and blue because for the past decade or so, the media have used these colours on election maps to indicate areas of Republican (red) and Democrat (blue) support – hence states being referred to as 'red states' or 'blue states'.

in Congress. A number of factors were said to have contributed towards this increase in partisanship:

- The shift of southern conservative Democrats to the Republican Party.
- The end of the Cold War consensus in foreign policy following the demise of the Soviet Union.
- The polarising presidencies of Bill Clinton (1993–2001) and George W. Bush (2001–09).
- The effect of the 'new media' such as direct mail, talk radio, cable television and the Internet.

Year	House: Democrats–Republicans	Senate: Democrats–Republicans	Governors: Democrats–Republicans
1960	99–7	22–0	11–0
1962	95–11	21–1	11–0
1964	89–17	21–1	11–0
1966	83–23	19–3	9–2
1968	80–26	18–4	9–2
1970	79–27	16–5	9–2
1972	77–31	14–7	8–3
1974	81–27	15–6	8–3
1976	80–28	16–5	9–2
1978	78–30	15–6	8–3
1980	69–39	11–10	6–5
1982	82–34	11–11	9–2
1984	80–36	12–10	8–3
1986	78–38	16–6	6–5
1988	77–39	15–7	6–5
1990	77–39	15–7	8–3
1992	77–48	13–9	8–3
1994	61–64	9–13	5–6
1996	54–71	7–15	5–6
1998	54–71	8–14	4–7
2000	53–71	9–13	5–6
2002	55–76	9–13	4–7
2004	49–82	4–18	4–7
2006	54–77	5–17	5–6
2008	59–72	7–15	4–7

Table 3.1 The break-up of the 'solid South', 1960–2008

B The two-party system

1 The facts

That the USA does have a **two-party system** is almost indisputable. Look at the following facts:

- Every president since 1856 has been either a Democrat or a Republican.
- In every presidential election since 1916, the combined Democrat and Republican vote has exceeded 80% of the total votes cast.
- In 21 of those last 25 presidential elections, the combined Democrat and Republican vote has exceeded 90% of the total votes cast, reaching 99% in both 1984 and 1988.

- In January 2009, every member of the US Senate belonged to one of the two major parties, except Senator Bernie Sanders of Vermont, who sits as an Independent, and Senator Joe Lieberman, an Independent Democrat.
- At the same time, all of the 435 members of the House of Representatives are either a Democrat or a Republican.
- Of the 50 state governors, all are either Democrats or Republicans.

The Democrats and Republicans dominate politics and elections in the USA to a startling extent.

> In the 2005 UK general election, the combined Labour and Conservative vote was just 67.5%.

> Following the 2005 UK general election, there were 91 members of the House of Commons (out of 646) who belonged to neither of the two major parties.

2 The reasons

There are two main reasons why the USA has a two-party system:

(1) The first-past-the-post, winner-takes-all electoral system.

(2) The diversity and all-embracing nature of the two major parties, which allows very little room for third parties.

But it could be argued that the USA does *not* have a two-party system, or that at least the picture is rather more complex than the statistics above would lead us to believe. Consider other analyses of the US party system.

3 Other analyses

Some commentators have suggested that the USA does not have a two-party system but a **fifty-party system**. Each individual state has its own party system.

> Also sometimes referred to as a '100-party system'.

Another analysis suggests that some states appear to have a **one-party system**. In such states, one party dominates to such an extent that the other seems hardly to exist. For example, Massachusetts is dominated by the Democratic Party. The Republicans have won the state in only one presidential election in the last 50 years, Reagan winning it by just 3,000 votes out of 2½ million in 1980. In Wyoming, it is the Republicans who, in that same period, have won all bar one presidential election (1964) and dominate the state at all levels.

Yet another analysis suggests that, because of the decline in the importance of political parties, the USA might be said to have a **no-party system**. Let us consider this a little more closely.

4 Theories of party decline

It was David Broder who popularised the idea that political parties in the USA were in serious decline. In the 1970s, he published a book with the title *The Party's Over*. Broder and others have put forward a number of reasons for concluding that the USA's parties were in serious decline:

- **Parties have lost control over presidential candidate selection.** With the rise in importance of presidential primaries (see Topic 2.A.2), parties no longer choose the candidates. This is now done by ordinary voters in the primaries.
- **Parties have been bypassed by federal 'matching funds' in presidential elections.** The 'matching funds' — introduced in the mid-1970s — are given to the candidates, not the parties (see Topic 2.A.5).
- **Television and opinion polls have bypassed parties as the medium by which candidates communicate with voters.** Party rallies and party-organised 'torch-light' processions etc. were the traditional way in which candidates spoke to and heard from voters. The party was therefore the most important vehicle of communication between politicians and voters. Nowadays, politicians increasingly talk to voters through the medium of television and voters 'talk back' through opinion polls.
- **Campaigns are more candidate-centred and issue-centred than they were.** Voters tend to vote more for a particular candidate, or because a candidate holds a certain view on a particular issue of importance to the voter (e.g. abortion, the environment, gun control), than for the party label. This has also shown itself in the rise of **'split-ticket' voting** (voting for candidates of different parties for different offices at the same election) and of 'independent' voters.

See also Topic 8.C.7 on abortion rights and Topic 8.C.3 on gun control.

5 Theories of party renewal

More recently, however, many commentators have been arguing that American political parties are undergoing renewal. What are the pointers to the theories of party renewal?

- **The party decline theories are somewhat exaggerated.** When all is said and done, it is still true that at the end of the twentieth century all the presidents elected in that century were either Democrats or Republicans; virtually all members of Congress were either Democrats or Republicans; even at the state level, the vast majority of state governors and state legislators were either Democrats or Republicans.
- **The parties have fought to regain some control over the presidential candidate selection process.** The Democratic Party introduced **super delegates** at their 1984 National Convention. These are professional, elected politicians who are given a vote at the Convention *ex officio*. By 2008, these super delegates accounted for almost 20% of the delegate votes at the Democratic National Convention. In 2000, it was possible to see how the

choice of the Republican Party 'establishment' — Governor George W. Bush — triumphed over the preferred choice of a significant number of rank-and-file Republican voters — Senator John McCain. The fact that Governor Bush enjoyed the almost unanimous support of the Republican Party hierarchy still counted for a lot even in a system dominated by presidential primaries. And in 2008, Democratic Party super delegates played a critical role in the choice of Barack Obama over Hillary Clinton in that year's presidential nomination race.

The Brock Reforms were named after Republican National Committee chairman Bill Brock.

- **Both parties have made significant strides in modernising their national party structures and network.** For the Republicans, the **Brock Reforms** significantly strengthened the standing of the Republican National Committee from the 1980s. And in the 1990s, Democratic National Committee chairman Charles Manatt did much the same for the Democrats, developing computerised direct mail facilities and a permanent headquarters in Washington DC.

Soft money can be defined as largely unregulated money given to national parties for such things as voter registration drives, the commissioning of opinion polls and issue-centred advertising.

- **The growth of 'soft money' in the 1980s and 1990s.** In an attempt to overcome the negative effects of 'matching funds' going directly to candidates rather than the parties, both major parties during the 1980s and 1990s took to raising large sums of 'soft money' which was entirely unregulated and led to new abuses. 'Soft money' was eventually banned by the Campaign Finance Reform Act (2002) known as the McCain–Feingold Act. (See Topic 2.A.5.)

- **Moves towards the 'nationalising' of campaigns.** Not only has this been seen increasingly in presidential elections, but it was also seen very dramatically in the 1994 mid-term congressional elections when the Republican Party launched its **Contract with America**. The brainchild of then Congressman Newt Gingrich, nearly all Republican House candidates in that election signed up to this ten-point contract. It promised, under a Republican-controlled Congress, that votes would be held within the first 100 days of such a Congress on ten policy issues of interest to conservative voters such as a balanced budget amendment and congressional term limits. But little of the Contract with America actually became law. In 2006, the Democrats had a national policy agenda for that year's mid-term elections entitled 'Six for 06' which accompanied their retaking control of both houses of Congress after 12 years in the minority.

For more details on 'party votes', see Topic 5.G.1.

- **Increased partisanship in Congress.** There has been some evidence that the 1990s saw increased levels of partisanship in Washington DC, especially during the Clinton administration. In 1995, the votes in Congress which were 'party votes' reached 73% in the House of Representatives, the highest figure since 1910. In the Senate the same year, 69% of votes were 'party votes', the highest since 1922. This came to a crescendo during the impeachment and trial of the President in 1998 and early 1999. The votes in the House of Representatives on the Articles of Impeachment were largely along party lines. Article I, accusing the President of perjury, was passed by 228 votes to 206. Only five Democrats voted 'yes' and only five Republicans voted 'no'. When this same Article was voted on in the Senate, the vote was 45 to 55. All those 45 senators voting 'guilty' on Article I were Republicans. Partisanship continued during the presidency of George W. Bush, especially over issues such as the war in Iraq, stem cell research and the State Child Health Insurance Programme (S-CHIP).

C Third parties

1 Types of third parties

There are a number of different types of third parties in the USA:
- national (e.g. Reform Party, Green Party, Libertarian Party, Natural Law Party)
- regional (e.g. George Wallace's American Independent Party — 1968)
- state (e.g. New York Conservative Party)
- permanent (e.g. Green Party, Libertarian Party)
- temporary (e.g. American Independent Party, Reform Party)
- issue-based (e.g. Green Party)
- ideological (e.g. Socialist Party, Constitution Party, Peace and Freedom Party)

Here are a few details to give you an idea of what some of these third parties stand for:
- **Constitution Party:** founded as the US Taxpayers' Party in 1992 and renamed in 1999, it is a collection of formerly separate right-wing independent parties. It is strongly anti-gun control, anti-tax, anti-immigration, protectionist, anti-United Nations, anti-gay rights, pro-school prayer and pro-life.
- **Green Party:** the informal US-affiliate of the European Greens. Ideologically on the left of US politics.
- **Libertarian Party:** stands for total individual liberty. It is pro-drug legalisation, pro-choice, pro-gay marriage, pro-home schooling and anti-gun control. It also stands for total economic freedom. The 1988 Libertarian Party presidential nominee Ron Paul is now a Republican Congressman from Texas.
- **Natural Law Party:** supports transcendental meditation, yogic flying and other peaceful 'New Age' practices as remedies for the problems of US society.
- **Peace and Freedom Party:** founded in the 1960s as a left-wing party opposed to the Vietnam War. Closely associated with the 'Black Panther' movement as well as Benjamin Spock, the well known baby doctor. Has links with the Workers' World Party.

Hence the claim, often made, that there are 'no third parties' in the USA.

What the USA does not have are national, permanent third parties that regularly win at least 5% of the popular vote in general elections, like the Liberal Democrats in the UK. US third parties are either national, permanent but insignificant (such as the Libertarian Party) or they are not national and permanent. Even Ross Perot's Reform Party, after impressive nationwide performances in 1992 and 1996, disintegrated in 2000. Table 3.2 shows the votes for third-party candidates in the 2008 presidential election. There are two things to note from this: first, the tiny proportion of votes attracted by such candidates; second, the fact that four of the six so-called third-party candidates were either current or former members of the two major parties: Republicans Bob Barr, Alan Keyes and Ron Paul, along with Democrat Cynthia McKinney. Barr and McKinney are both former members of Congress, Keyes is a perennial contestant in the Republican presidential primaries, whilst Paul is an incumbent Republican House member from Texas.

Candidate	Party	Popular votes	% of popular vote	Electoral College votes
Ralph Nader	Various	658,393	0.32	0
Bob Barr	Libertarian	489,661	0.24	0
Chuck Baldwin	Various	175,048	0.08	0
Cynthia McKinney	Green	143,160	0.07	0
Alan Keyes	American Independent	35,105	0.02	0
Ron Paul	Constitution	19,583	0.01	0

Table 3.2 Third-party support in the 2008 presidential election

2 Recent success by third parties

In recent presidential elections, third parties have enjoyed some success, as is shown in Table 3.3.

Year	Candidate	Party	% of popular vote	Electoral College votes
1968	George Wallace	American Independent	13	46
1980	John Anderson	National Unity	7	0
1992	Ross Perot	(No party affiliation)	19	0
1996	Ross Perot	Reform	9	0

Table 3.3 Significant third-party support in presidential elections (more than 5% of the popular vote) since 1968

Third parties have had very limited representation in Congress, as is shown in Table 3.4. They don't do much better when it comes to elections for state governors, as Table 3.5 shows.

Years	House/Senate	Name	Party	State
1971–77	Senate	James Buckley	New York Conservative	New York
1993–	House/Senate	Bernie Sanders	Independent	Vermont
July–October 1999	Senate	Bob Smith	US Taxpayers	New Hampshire
2000–02	House	Virgil Goode	Independent	Virginia
2001–06	Senate	James Jeffords	Independent	Vermont
2007-	Senate	Joe Lieberman	Independent Democrat	Connecticut

Table 3.4 Third-party members of Congress since 1971

Virgil Goode became a Republican in 2003.

Senator James Jeffords of Vermont switched from the Republican Party to be an Independent in May 2001.

Years	Name	Party	State
1975–79	James Longley	Independent	Maine
1991–95	Walter Hickel	Alaska Independent	Alaska
1991–95	Lowell Weicker	A Connecticut Party	Connecticut
1995–2003	Angus King	Independent	Maine
1999–2003	Jesse Ventura	Reform	Minnesota

Table 3.5 Third-party state governors since 1975

3 Difficulties facing third parties

In 1992, Ross Perot stood as a person rather than a party. He formed the Reform Party after his 1992 success. Hence one can talk of third party and 'independent' candidates to distinguish between the two.

The Reform Party did not get matching funds in 2004, having gained less than 1% of the vote in 2000.

Third parties in the USA face a number of significant difficulties:

- **The electoral system:** the first-past the post, winner-takes-all system, which is used for every election in the USA — federal, state and local — makes life very difficult for third parties. For example, Ross Perot won 19% of the vote in 1992 but won no Electoral College votes. This is particularly true of national third parties. Regional third parties fare better; see, for example, George Wallace in 1968.
- **Federal campaign finance laws:** the way candidates can qualify for 'matching funds' puts third-party candidates at a disadvantage. Major party candidates qualify by raising at least $5,000 in contributions of $250 or less in at least 20 states. But third-party candidates qualify only by getting at least 5% of the popular vote. Not only is this a difficult hurdle, but it means that the party can qualify only in the next round of elections. Hence Ross Perot could not qualify for matching funds in 1992, but his Reform Party did qualify in 1996 and 2000 by virtue of getting more than 5% in the previous election.
- **State ballot access laws:** the way third-party candidates have to qualify to get their names on the ballot paper in each state makes life very difficult for third parties. States require third-party candidates to present a petition signed by a certain number of registered voters in the state. Whilst Tennessee requires only 25 signatures, in Montana the figure is 5% of all registered voters. This takes time and money. In 1980, John Anderson estimated that to get his name on the ballot in all 50 states, he had to collect around 1.2 million signatures nationwide and that he spent over $3 million in doing so.
- **Lack of resources:** third-party candidates are generally very short of resources — especially financial resources. They find fundraising difficult. People are reluctant to give money to parties they see as sure losers, creating something of a 'catch 22' situation.
- **Lack of media coverage:** third parties also tend to miss out on media coverage. Newspapers and television virtually ignore them. They cannot afford much if anything in the way of TV advertisements. They are generally excluded from the televised presidential debates.
- **Lack of well-known, well-qualified candidates:** again something of a self-fulfilling prophecy. Third-party candidates are unlikely to be household names and are unlikely to have held any significant political office.

Ross Perot's inclusion in 1992 is the only exception

- **Regarded as too ideological:** because the two major parties are so all-embracing in their ideologies, third parties are often left only the ideological fringes of the political spectrum — the Constitution Party or the Socialist Party. Others are easily linked to 'extremism' by their opponents. The following slogan, for example, was used against third-party candidate Governor George Wallace during his 1968 presidential campaign: 'If you liked Hitler, you'll love Wallace'.
- **The tactics of the two major parties:** if a third-party candidate does still manage to win significant support (e.g. Wallace in 1968, Perot in 1992), one or both of the two major parties will eventually adopt some of their policies. So, for example, Nixon pursued what he called his 'southern strategy' in 1972 to woo ex-Wallace voters. Both Governor Clinton and President Bush addressed the federal budget deficit issue in the 1992 campaign after Ross Perot had got so much support by talking about it. In this sense, third parties can be seen to be the 'winners' — losing the election but winning the policy debate.

Examiners sometimes hint at this when they ask questions such as 'Examine the claim that third parties always lose in presidential elections.'

Questions

1 How do the Northeast and west coast differ ideologically from the South?

2 What four factors have been suggested as contributing to increased partisanship?

3 What facts suggest that the USA has a two-party system?

4 What two reasons are given for the USA having a two-party system?

5 What is meant by the term 'fifty-party system'?

6 What four factors suggest party decline in the USA?

7 What five factors suggest party renewal in the USA?

8 What was the 'Contract with America'?

9 Give three examples of third parties in the USA.

10 What difficulties do third parties face in USA politics?

Pressure groups are regarded as having important implications for a modern democracy. Through them, citizens can participate in the political process between elections. They can also use their membership of them to pressurise all three branches of government — the legislature (Congress), the executive (the president and the bureaucracy) and the judiciary, including the Supreme Court. In a country like the USA, with a participatory tradition and a more open form of government than in the UK, pressure groups seem to take on added importance. But are pressure groups always 'good' for democracy?

The topic is divided into eight major headings:

A Definition

B Types of pressure groups

C Functions of pressure groups

D Reasons for joining pressure groups

E Methods used by pressure groups

F Importance of pressure groups

G Pressure group activity

H Influence on the federal government

I Arguments for and against pressure groups

A Definition

A pressure group is an organised interest group in which members share and actively pursue common views and objectives to influence government. Pressure groups are therefore quite distinct from political parties. Whereas political parties seek to **win control of government**, pressure groups seek to **influence** those who have won control of government.

Thus the Green Party is different from Greenpeace.

Pressure groups vary considerably in terms of size, wealth and influence. Pressure groups in the USA operate at all levels of government — federal, state and local — and seek to bring their influence to bear on all three branches of government — the legislature, the executive and the judiciary.

B Types of pressure groups

Robert McKeever has come up with a very helpful typology of interest groups and this is shown in Table 4.1 on page 62.

Type	Example
Business/trade	American Business Conference National Association of Manufacturers National Automobile Dealers Association
Agriculture	American Farm Bureau Federation National Farmers' Union Associated Milk Producers Inc.
Unions	American Federation of Labor–Congress of Industrial Organisations (AFL–CIO) United Auto Workers
Professional	American Medical Association National Education Association American Bar Association
Single issue	Mothers Against Drunk Driving (MADD) National Rifle Association (NRA) National Abortion and Reproductive Rights Action League
Ideological	American Conservative Union People for the American Way American Civil Liberties Union (ACLU)
Group rights	National Association for the Advancement of Colored People (NAACP) National Organisation for Women (NOW) American Association of Retired Persons
Public interest	Common Cause Friends of the Earth

Table 4.1 Pressure groups: types and examples

C Functions of pressure groups

Pressure groups are said to have five basic functions:

(1) **Representation** — they represent the interests of various groups in society. Table 4.1 gives some examples of the types of groups that pressure groups can represent in American politics.

(2) **Citizen participation** — they increase the opportunities for ordinary citizens to participate in the decision-making process between elections.

(3) **Public education** — they attempt to educate public opinion, warning them of dangers if issues are not addressed. One can see this being done by pressure groups operating in such issue areas as the environment and gun control.

(4) **Agenda building** — they attempt to influence the agendas of political parties, legislators and bureaucracies to give prominence and priority to their interests. They will attempt to bring together different parts of American society — for example business groups, religious groups, state governments, professional organisations — to work together to achieve a common interest.

(5) **Programme monitoring** — they will scrutinise and hold government to account in the implementation of policies to try to ensure that promises are fulfilled, policies are actually 'delivered' and regulations are enforced.

D Reasons for joining pressure groups

Berry and Wilcox (*The Interest Group Society*, 2007) suggest three different classes of benefit which go some way to explaining why Americans join pressure groups.

(1) **Material benefits:** people join pressure groups because they think that either they personally, or society as a whole, will gain some material benefit as a result. Material benefits range from the personal ones a member gains from joining a group to the policy changes it offers.

(2) **Purposive benefits:** people join pressure groups to be part of a movement or a cause to try to make society, or even the world, a better place. Membership of this kind has a certain 'feel good' factor about it for those joining.

(3) **Solidarity benefits:** people join pressure groups to interact with like-minded people, taking part in group activities.

E Methods used by pressure groups

Pressure groups use four principal methods to fulfil their functions.

(1) **Electioneering and endorsement.** Campaign finance reform has meant that significant changes have taken place in the electioneering and fundraising roles of pressure groups. The 1970s reforms encouraged the setting up of Political Action Committees (PACs) — organisations whose purpose is to raise and then give campaign funds to candidates for political office. There is a clear trend that incumbents attract more PAC money than challengers. Pressure groups endorse or oppose candidates for political office based on the candidates' position on the policy areas of concern to them. At election time, groups will often publish voter guides on their websites showing which candidates most closely support the group's stand on issues.

(2) **Lobbying.** Lobbying is an attempt to exert influence on the policy-making process, in any of the three branches of government, by individuals or organised groups. In order to facilitate lobbying, many groups have offices in Washington DC, state capitals and other major US cities. In Washington DC, the lobbyist firms are collectively known as the 'K Street corridor' — named after the street in the city where many lobbyists have their offices. Lobbyists provide policy-makers with information. And for members of

Congress, they may also provide them with important voting cues. Many lobbying firms recruit former policy-makers through what is known as 'the revolving door syndrome'.

(3) **Publicity.** Lobbying firms launch public relations campaigns to influence the policy-making process. Both the Clinton and Bush presidencies felt the effect of powerful lobbying firms launching publicity blitzes against some of their flagship policies — healthcare and social security reform, to name but two. Publicity campaigns are waged through a number of different means such as television advertisements, journal advertising, roadside hoardings, bumper stickers or badges.

(4) **Organising grassroots activities.** These include such activities as postal blitzes on members of Congress, the White House or a government department, marches and demonstrations. Most are peaceful, but some may resort to violence.

F Importance of pressure groups

But why are pressure groups so important in American politics, more important than in the UK for example? Here are three important reasons for this:

(1) **America is a very diverse and heterogeneous society.** America has been described as a 'melting pot', conveying the picture of all types of diverse groups of people mixed together. The more diverse a society is, the greater will be the variety of special interests to represent. One can see this immediately in the racial mix of American society. Another term used to refer to America is that it is the 'hyphenated society'. Everyone seems to have a prefix to their being an 'American', whether it be 'African-American', 'Cuban-American', 'Polish-American', 'Irish-American' or even 'Native-American'. And each one has its own pressure group. There are said to be almost 100 different religions that claim at least 50,000 members each. Again, here are more interests and groups to represent. And, as we saw at the beginning of Topic 1, America is a vast country spread over different regions, all with their own cultures and traditions.

(2) **The American political system has a great many access points.** In the UK, political power is quite highly centralised. There are few access points for the ordinary citizen to influence government. The executive branch (prime minister and cabinet) largely controls the legislature (Parliament). Parliament is made up of only one truly effective chamber (the House of Commons). The prime minister, it could be argued, exercises a good deal of relatively unchecked power. Hence there are few points at which real political decisions are made and there are, therefore, few access points. But in the USA there is a doctrine of 'shared powers' (see Topic 1.C) — shared between the three branches of the federal government as well as between

the federal government and the state governments. Even an institution like Congress is very fragmented. It is not just on the floors of two chambers where decisions are made, but in the numerous committee rooms as well. Hence there are many points at which real political decisions are made. There are, therefore, many access points.

(3) **The weakness of political parties in America means that citizens turn more to pressure groups.** In a country such as the UK, which has strong, centralised, disciplined political parties, these parties are seen as the principal vehicles for political activity. Also in the UK, where one party will dominate the government by controlling both the executive and legislative branches of government, parties are seen as more able to deliver their promises and policy proposals. In a country such as the USA, which has relatively weak, decentralised and undisciplined political parties, parties are not seen in this light. And as we also know, these days it is quite unlikely that any one party will control (in any sense of the word) both the executive and legislative branches of the federal government. Democrat Bill Clinton enjoyed party control of Congress for only 2 of his 8 years in office; Republican George W. Bush for 4½ of his 8 years.

G Pressure group activity

In recent decades, American pressure groups have been especially important in policy areas such as:

1 Environmental protection

Towards the end of the nineteenth century, as both industrialisation and 'westward expansion' were well under way, the matter of environmental conservation became important. This is when the Sierra Club was formed. This was followed in the early twentieth century by the Wilderness Society and the National Wildlife Federation. Such groups have been behind the push towards stricter laws for environmental protection.

2 Civil rights for African-Americans

The National Association for the Advancement of Colored People (NAACP) was the force behind the landmark Supreme Court decision of *Brown v. the Board of Education of Topeka* (1954) (see Topic 8.C.6) as well as the subsequent passage of much civil rights legislation. The NAACP would use its money and professional expertise to bring cases to court for people who could not otherwise afford it. These would be cases which the NAACP believed it could win and which would benefit the interests of African-Americans. The NAACP has continued to be at the centre of political debate in America over affirmative action programmes.

See also Topic 9.

3 Women's rights

Groups such as the League of Women Voters and the National Organization for Women pushed — unsuccessfully — for the passage of an Equal Rights Amendment to the Constitution during the 1970s and 1980s. But they have remained very active in American politics, campaigning on such issues as equal pay and job opportunities for women. They have also been involved in the debate over attempting to root out sexual harassment in the workplace, with some high-profile cases in the United States military. This latter issue also received much public debate concerning President Clinton's relationships with women such as Paula Corbin Jones. Some criticised women's groups for not being more critical of the President. Women's groups have also been very much involved in the abortion debate, as well as trying to increase the number of women elected to Congress. The pressure group EMILY's List supports female candidates, helping them to raise money early on in the electoral cycle.

4 Abortion rights

'Pro-choice' = in favour of a woman's right (to choose) to have an abortion; 'pro-life' = anti-abortion.

Both the pro-choice and pro-life lobbies have been very active in American politics during the past three to four decades. Since the 1973 *Roe v. Wade* decision by the Supreme Court (see Topic 8.C.7), pro-choice groups have fought to preserve the constitutional right of women to have an abortion, whereas the pro-life groups have fought to have it both narrowed and overturned. Most recently, they have been involved in the debate concerning the practice of so-called 'partial birth abortions'. When Congress tried to ban such types of abortion, President Clinton vetoed the bills, once in 1996 and again in 1997. In 2000, the Supreme Court refused to allow states to ban these types of abortion. But in 2007, the Supreme Court upheld the ban, declaring it to be constitutional.

You will find details and other examples of presidential vetoes in Topic 6.A.4.

5 Gun control

The National Rifle Association (NRA) is arguably one of the most powerful interest groups in American politics, with a membership of some 3 million. It was formed in 1871 as a group dedicated to teaching people how to use guns. But since the 1960s, it has been very influential in stopping what it sees as encroachments on citizens' rights to own and use legal firearms. It seeks to uphold the strictest interpretation of the Second Amendment right to 'keep and bear arms'. It also works to oppose tougher gun control laws put forward at any level of government. The NRA has opposed the passage of the **Brady Bill** and the assault weapons ban, as well as laws requiring background checks on those purchasing guns and the mandatory sale of trigger locks with handguns. The NRA also played an important role in the Supreme Court case of *District of Columbia v. Heller* (2008), in which the Court declared unconstitutional the law banning the ownership of handguns in the District.

Named after James Brady, President Reagan's Press Secretary, who was shot and seriously wounded during the assassination attempt on the President in March 1981.

H Influence on the federal government

Pressure groups attempt to influence Congress, the federal bureaucracy and the courts. American government has far more 'access points' than does government in the UK. Government is thought to be more 'open'. This enhances the potential for influence by pressure groups. And in a system where political parties are clearly weaker than they are in the UK, this again increases opportunities for pressure groups to have greater degrees of influence.

1 *Influence on the legislature*

Also see Topic 5.G.4.

Pressure groups seek to influence the way House and Senate members vote. They do this by a number of methods, including:

- direct contact with House and Senate members and their senior staff
- direct contact with the relevant House and Senate committee members and their staff

Americans do far more of this than their UK counterparts.

- organising constituents to write to, phone, fax, e-mail or visit their House and Senate members to express their support for or opposition to a certain policy initiative
- publicising the voting records of House and Senate members
- endorsement of supportive members and opposition to non-supportive members in forthcoming re-election campaigns
- fundraising, campaigning for or against members of Congress — paying for radio/television advertisements etc.

Pressure groups may also launch high-profile campaigns in the media when a significant piece of legislation is about to come up for a crucial debate and vote in Congress. Recent examples include congressional debates and votes on healthcare reform, welfare reform, gun control and international environmental agreements.

2 *Influence on the executive*

Pressure groups will seek to maintain strong ties with relevant executive departments, agencies and regulatory commissions. This is especially the case when it comes to the regulatory work of the federal government — regulations, for example, regarding health and safety at work, business, the transport and communications industries or the environment.

Problems can emerge when regulatory bodies are thought to have too cosy a relationship with the particular group they are meant to be regulating. Are they acting as 'watch dogs' or 'lap dogs'?

Edward Ashbee and Nigel Ashford (*US Politics Today*, Manchester University Press, 1999) identify another close link: that between what they call 'producer' groups — such as companies, labour unions or small business federations — and relevant government departments and agencies seeking protection, funding, subsidies or price guarantee mechanisms.

3 ### *Influence on the judiciary*

*Amicus curiae =
'friend of the court'.*

Pressure groups can hope to influence the courts by offering *amicus curiae* briefings. Through these, pressure groups will have an opportunity to present their views to the court in writing before oral arguments are heard. Pressure groups have certainly used this to great effect in recent decades in such areas as the civil rights of racial minorities, abortion rights and First Amendment rights. They may also sponsor cases to come before the courts, as the NAACP did in the 1954 *Brown v. Board* case. They may actually bring cases themselves, such as the 2005 *McCreary v. American Civil Liberties Union* case.

In the last 20 years, pressure groups have also been very active in supporting or opposing the nomination of judges, especially those to the Supreme Court. They were certainly very active in the Senate confirmation hearings surrounding Robert Bork (1987) and Clarence Thomas (1991), as well as those of John Roberts (2005) and Samuel Alito (2006).

▎Arguments for and against pressure groups

Arguments in favour of pressure groups having an important role to play in American politics stress that pressure groups provide useful functions, by acting as:
- information-givers — to members of Congress, government departments, the courts and the electorate as a whole, for whom they play an 'educating' role
- policy formulators
- a 'sounding board' for members of Congress and government departments
- enhancers of political participation, especially between elections and on specific issues

Senator Edward Kennedy once commented that America has 'the finest Congress that money can buy'.

Arguments against pressure groups having as much power as they currently seem to have in American politics include the following:
- Money becomes the all-deciding factor — you have to 'pay to play'.
- They work too much for 'special' interests and against the 'national' interests.
- They tend to be élitist and largely unaccountable, and their power thereby detracts from elected (Congress) and accountable (executive) officials.
- They lead to inequalities of power, for example in policy debates relating to healthcare, tobacco and gun control.

- The 'revolving door syndrome' allows former members of Congress or the executive branch to take up highly paid jobs as lobbyists. This may mean that federal officials use their position to do favours in exchange for an attractive post when they leave office.
- They sometimes use methods of 'direct action' that are deemed by others to be inappropriate, for example methods used recently by animal rights groups, pro- and anti-abortion groups, environmentalists and anti-capitalist groups.

Questions

1 **(a)** Define a pressure group. **(b)** How does it differ from a political party?

2 Give four examples of different types of pressure groups.

3 What are the five functions of pressure groups?

4 Give three reasons why people join pressure groups.

5 Give four methods used by pressure groups.

6 Give three reasons why pressure groups are important in the USA.

7 How do pressure groups seek to influence Congress?

8 How can pressure groups influence the courts?

9 Give four arguments in favour of pressure groups.

10 Give four arguments against pressure groups.

We now move on to look at the three branches of the federal government — the legislature (Congress), the executive (the president) and the judiciary (the Supreme Court). As we saw in Topic 1, they are the branches dealt with by the first three Articles of the Constitution — Congress (Article I), the president (Article II) and the Supreme Court (Article III). Topic 5 looks at Congress, which, as the legislative branch, makes the laws. We need to know about and understand its membership, election, powers and organisation. We need to know what it does and how it does it. We also need to remember that in US politics, checks and balances are never far away. So we shall need to keep an eye out for how Congress relates to the other two branches of government.

The topic is divided into eight major headings:

A Membership

B Powers

C Comparison between the House and the Senate

D Leadership

E The committee system

F The legislative process

G Voting in Congress

H Oversight of the executive branch

A Membership

1 Terminology

Congress is the overall name for both houses. Congress is made up of two houses — the House of Representatives and the Senate. Congress is therefore described as **bicameral** — made up of two houses or 'chambers'. There is potential confusion in the terms used to refer to members of each house. The problem lies in the fact that although the term 'Congress' refers to *both* houses, the term 'Congressman' refers only to members of the House of Representatives. Members of the Senate are called 'senators'.

2 House membership

In the House of Representatives there are 435 members. Each state has a certain number of members proportional to the population of the state. Except in states that have just one House member, each member represents a sub-division of the state known as a 'District'. By the time of the 2002 elections, California (the largest state) had 53, Wyoming (the smallest state) just one. As we have already seen (Topic 2.B), members are elected for **2-year terms** and the Constitution states that to be a member of the House of Representatives you must:

- be at least 25 years of age
- have been a US citizen for at least 7 years
- be a resident of the state in which your District is situated

In the House of Representatives at the beginning of the 111th Congress (January 2009), amongst the 435 members there were:

- 75 women
- 39 African-Americans
- 23 Hispanics
- 152 lawyers
- 132 Roman Catholics
- no ex-senators

The last ex-senator in the House was Claude Pepper of Florida, who served in the Senate 1936–50 but lost in a primary. He then served in the House from 1962 until his death in 1989.

Years	Women	African-Americans
1991–92	28	25
1993–94	47	38
1995–96	48	38
1997–98	51	38
1999–2000	56	35
2001–02	59	36
2003–04	59	38
2005–06	64	41
2007–08	71	40
2009–10	75	39

Table 5.1 Women and African-American members of the House since 1991

As Table 5.1 shows, the number of women and African-American members in the House has increased quite significantly over the past 30 years. This was particularly the case following the elections in 1992. But the 75 women members at the start of the 111th Congress (2009–10) still represent only 17% of the membership, well below the percentage they make up of the US electorate. For African-Americans, the 39 members represent 9%, only slightly below their 10% in society as a whole.

The Democrats dubbed 1992 'the year of the woman'.

3 *Senate membership*

In the Senate there are 100 members. Each state — regardless of population — has two senators. Each senator represents the entire state. They are elected for **6-year terms. One-third of the Senate is up for re-election every 2 years**. Senate elections are held on the same day as elections to the House.

The Constitution states that to be a senator you must:

- be at least 30 years of age
- have been a US citizen for at least 9 years
- be a resident of the state you represent

In the Senate at the beginning of the 111th Congress (January 2009), amongst the 100 members there were:

- 17 women
- 1 African-American
- 2 Hispanics
- 54 lawyers
- 24 Roman Catholics
- 48 ex-House members

Again, as in the House, the number of women members has increased of late but still stands at a proportionately low number (see Table 5.2). Following the defeat of Democrat Carol Moseley Braun of Illinois in 1998, there were no African-American senators until the election of Barack Obama in 2004. Following his election as president, the Illinois state governor appointed another African-American, Roland Burris, to fill the vacancy. It is highly significant that just under half (48) of the current Senate are former members of the House of Representatives. It is an important indicator of the perceived power and prestige of the Senate in comparison to the House.

Years	Women	African-Americans
1991–92	2	0
1993–94	7	1
1995–96	8	1
1997–98	9	1
1999–2000	9	0
2001–02	13	0
2003–04	14	0
2005–06	14	1
2007–08	16	1
2009–10	17	1

Table 5.2 Women and African-American members of the Senate since 1991

B Powers

In terms of powers, each house has **exclusive powers** and **joint powers**. In other words, each house has powers that they alone — and not the other house — possess. Equally, each house shares powers with the other house.

1 Exclusive powers

The House of Representatives has three exclusive powers:

(1) To begin consideration of all money bills.

The term 'impeachment' is often misunderstood. It simply means to make a formal accusation against someone.

Senator William Blount was accused in 1797 of 'aiding the British'! Supreme Court Justice Samuel Chase was accused in 1804 of making 'harsh, partisan and unfair' decisions.

(2) To impeach any member of the executive or judicial branches of the federal government.

(3) To elect the president if the Electoral College is deadlocked.

The Founding Fathers gave the House of Representatives **the power to begin consideration of all money bills** because it was the only directly elected chamber at that time.

Impeachment means 'making a formal accusation' or 'bringing charges' against any member of the other two branches. We saw this in 1998, when the House of Representatives impeached President Clinton on two counts — perjury and obstruction of justice. President Clinton was the seventeenth person to be impeached by the House since the first case in 1797, but only the second president. President Andrew Johnson was impeached — and acquitted by the Senate — in 1868. Other than two presidents, those impeached have included:

- 1 senator
- 1 Supreme Court justice
- 2 Cabinet members
- 11 District (trial court) judges

The third power — **to elect the president if the Electoral College is deadlocked** — is now almost redundant, not having been used since 1824.

The Senate has four exclusive powers:

(1) To ratify all treaties negotiated by the president — **a two-thirds majority required**.

(2) To confirm many appointments (to the executive and judicial branches) made by the president — **a simple majority required**.

(3) To try cases of impeachment — **a two-thirds majority required** to convict.

(4) To elect the vice-president if the Electoral College is deadlocked.

It is the first two of these exclusive powers that go some way to making the Senate the more powerful and prestigious of the two chambers.

Only the Senate has the power to **ratify treaties and confirm appointments**. Although the Senate usually agrees, remember that presidents will generally only submit those treaties and appointments that they know the Senate will approve. Thus the Senate has a kind of hidden power. In 1999, the Senate rejected the Comprehensive Test Ban Treaty. The vote was 48–51, 18 votes short of the two-thirds majority required. The same year, the Senate rejected President Clinton's nomination of Ronnie White to be a judge on the federal trial court. The vote here was 45–54, 5 votes short of the simple majority required.

Once the House has impeached someone, the Senate **tries that case of impeachment**. To find that person guilty, two-thirds of the senators voting must vote 'guilty'. In the votes on the two charges brought against President Clinton, the Senate voted 45–55 and 50–50, respectively 22 and 17 votes short of the two-thirds majority required. The last person to be found guilty by the Senate — and thus removed from office — was District Court Judge Walter Nixon. He was impeached and found guilty of perjury in 1989.

The final exclusive Senate power — **to elect the vice-president if the Electoral College is deadlocked** — remains unused since 1824.

2 | *Joint powers*

Together, the House of Representatives and the Senate have five joint powers:

(1) To pass legislation, including the budget.

(2) To conduct investigations regarding the actions of the executive branch.

(3) To initiate constitutional amendments.

(4) To declare war.

(5) To confirm the appointment of a newly appointed vice-president.

> Notice that they confirm only a newly appointed vice-president, not one who is elected.

It is very important to remember that the House and the Senate share arguably the most important power of Congress, that of **passing legislation**. Unlike in the UK Parliament, where the House of Commons dominates the legislative process, in the US Congress the two chambers have equal legislative power. This can be seen in the following ways:

- All legislation must pass through all stages in **both houses**.
- **Both houses** conduct detailed scrutiny of legislation in committee.
- **Both houses** have full power of amendment over all bills, usually resulting in there being two different versions of the same bill once it has gone through both houses.
- Conference committees — set up to reconcile the two different versions of the same bill — are made up of members of **both houses** and their decisions must be agreed to by **both houses**.
- It takes a two-thirds majority in **both houses** to override a presidential veto.

Both houses have standing committees, which can conduct investigations of the work of the executive branch. Both houses can also establish select committees to perform the same function.

In order **to propose an amendment to the Constitution**, a two-thirds majority is required in both houses (see Topic 1.B.4).

The joint power to **declare war** has become somewhat redundant. The power has not been used since December 1941, when Congress declared war on Japan following the attack on Pearl Harbor. That was the fifth time it had been used, the others being:

> This was against Great Britain.

- the war of 1812
- the Mexican war in 1848
- the Spanish–American war in 1898
- the First World War in 1917

> This related to matters when Agnew was Governor of Maryland.

The final joint power is relatively new, having been granted in 1967 by the 25th Amendment. Should the office of the vice-presidency become vacant between elections, the president is now empowered to nominate a new vice-president to fill the vacancy. But the nomination must be confirmed by a simple majority vote in both houses of Congress. The power has been used twice — in 1973 and 1974. In 1973, Vice-President Spiro Agnew resigned after pleading 'no contest' to a charge of income tax evasion. President Nixon appointed the Republican (Minority) Leader of the House of Representatives Gerald Ford as his new vice-president. Ford was confirmed by the Senate by 92 votes to 3, and by the House 387–35.

Less than a year later, President Nixon resigned and Ford became president, again leaving the vice-presidency vacant. Ford chose former New York Governor Nelson Rockefeller. Rockefeller was easily confirmed in the Senate (90–7) but found things tougher in the House (287–128).

C Comparison between the House and the Senate

Having looked at the membership and powers of both houses, let us compare the two houses. It is often suggested that the Senate is more powerful and prestigious than the House. Is this the case? There is a 'yes' and a 'no' answer.

Reasons why the Senate is often thought of as being more prestigious and powerful than the House of Representatives are:

This has been a frequent focus for A-level questions. Too many candidates forget to argue the 'no' side.

- Senators **represent the entire state**, not just part of the state.
- Senators **serve 6-year terms**, three times as long as House members.
- As a senator you are **one of 100**, rather than one of 435.
- Senators are therefore **likely to chair a committee** much sooner in their career than their House counterparts.
- Senators often enjoy much **greater name recognition**, not only in their state but often across the nation as a whole.
- **House members frequently seek election to the Senate**; the reverse is almost unknown.

In January 2009, there were 48 ex-House members in the Senate but no ex-senators in the House.

- Senators are more frequently **thought of as likely presidential candidates**. Recent examples include Senators Barack Obama (D), Hillary Clinton (D), Chris Dodd (D), Joe Biden (D), John McCain (R) and Sam Brownback (R), all of whom contested their party's presidential nomination race in 2008.
- Senators are **more frequently nominated as vice-presidential running-mates**. Recent examples include Senators Joe Lieberman (2000), John Edwards (2004) and Joe Biden (2008) — all Democrats.
- Senators have **exclusive powers**, including the ratification of treaties and the confirmation of appointments, which are generally agreed to be more significant than the exclusive powers enjoyed by House members.

However, it is also important to remember that in some ways Senate and House members are equal. The most important argument here concerns the equality of the two houses in the legislative process:

- All bills must go through all stages **in both houses**; neither can overturn the decisions of the other.
- **Both houses** have powerful standing committees, which conduct separate hearings at the all-important committee stage.
- At the conference committee stage, **members of both houses** are represented.
- **Both houses** must agree to the compromise reached at the conference committee.
- To override a presidential veto, a two-thirds majority in **both houses** is required.

	Senate	House
Number of members	100	435
Number per state	2	Proportional to population
Length of term	6 years	2 years
Age qualification	30	25
Citizenship qualification	9 years	7 years
Average age	63	56
Presiding officer	Vice-president	Speaker
Number of women	17	75
Number of African-Americans	1	39
Ex-members of other house	48	0
Special powers	(i) Ratify treaties (ii) Confirm appointments (iii) Try cases of impeachment (iv) Elect vice-president if Electoral College is deadlocked	(i) Initiate money bills (ii) Impeachment (iii) Elect president if Electoral College is deadlocked
Joint powers	(i) Legislation (ii) Declare war (iii) Initiate constitutional amendments (iv) Confirm newly appointed vice-president	

Table 5.3 Senate and House compared

D Leadership

Currently Nancy Pelosi, a Democrat from California, first elected as Speaker in 2007.

The main leadership posts in Congress are:
- the Speaker of the House of Representatives
- the Majority and Minority Leaders of both houses
- standing committee chairs

1 Speaker of the House of Representatives

The Speaker of the House of Representatives is:
- elected by the entire House membership at the beginning of each new Congress (i.e. every 2 years)
- usually the nominee of the majority party in the House at the time
- not required by the Constitution to be a serving member of the House, though all Speakers have been
- next in line to the presidency after the vice-president, but this is less significant with the passage of the 25th Amendment requiring the vice-presidency to be filled if a vacancy should occur there

Unlike the Speaker of the House of Commons, the Speaker of the House of Representatives is a political player, not just a neutral umpire. In essence, the

Speaker is the leader of the majority party in the House and, if of a different party from the president, may act as the major spokesperson for the party, a kind of 'leader of the opposition'.

The Speaker has the following powers and functions:
- acts as the presiding officer of the House
- interprets and enforces the rules of the House, decides points of order
- refers bills to committees
- appoints select and conference committee chairs
- appoints majority party members of the House Rules Committee
- may exercise considerable influence in the flow of legislation through the House, as well as in committee assignments for majority party members and even the selection of House standing committee chairs

Some Speakers have become politicians of considerable stature and importance. Recent examples would include Democrat Tip O'Neill and Republican Newt Gingrich. Others, such as Dennis Hastert, have been more low-key.

That is, chairs debates.

This was certainly true of Newt Gingrich (Speaker 1995–98).

2 *Majority and Minority Leaders*

In both the House and the Senate, there is a Majority and Minority Leader. They are elected by their respective party groups in each house every 2 years at the start of each Congress.

In both houses, the Majority and Minority Leaders:
- act as day-by-day 'directors of operations' on the floor of their respective houses
- hold press briefings to talk about their party's policy agenda
- act as liaison between the House/Senate and the White House
- in the Senate, make **unanimous consent agreements** to bring bills for debate on the Senate floor (see F.3)

In the House, the Majority Leader plays a 'number two' role to the Speaker. The Majority and Minority Leaders may hope to become Speaker. Most Speakers — though not Dennis Hastert — previously held one of these two posts.

E The committee system

There are many different types of committee in both houses of Congress. The most important are:
- standing committees
- the House Rules Committee
- conference committees
- select committees

1 *Standing committees*

1.1 Membership

'Standing' = permanent.

Standing committees exist in both houses of Congress. They are **permanent, policy specialist committees**. There are 16 in each house. In the House there are also two rather different standing committees — the House Rules Committee, which timetables bills on the House floor (see E.2), and the Standards of Official Conduct Committee, which deals with the professional and ethical conduct of House members. Most standing committees are divided into subcommittees. So, for example, one of the subcommittees of the House Science and Technology Committee is the Energy and Environment Subcommittee, whilst the subcommittees of the Senate Armed Services Committee include one on Seapower and another on Strategic Forces.

A typical Senate standing committee has around 18 members on it, whilst a typical House standing committee is made up of around 45–50 members.

The party balance in each standing committee is in the same proportion to that which exists within the chamber as a whole. In the House of Representatives at the beginning of the 111th Congress (January 2009), the Democrats had a 257–178 advantage over the Republicans. So the 46-member House Agriculture Committee had a 28–18 Democrat–Republican balance. In the Senate, the party split was 57–41, with two Independents. So the 26-member Senate Armed Services Committee had a 15–11 split between Democrats and Republicans.

Standing committee chairs are always drawn from the majority party in that particular house. Thus in January 2009, all House and Senate standing committee chairs were Democrats. The **seniority rule** states that the chair of a standing committee will be the member of the majority party with the **longest continuous service on that committee**. Referred to by its critics as the 'senility rule', it has now been relaxed, especially in the House of Representatives. Also in the House, the Republicans imposed 6-year limits on the tenure of all standing committee chairs from January 1995. This resulted in 14 House standing committees having a new chair in January 2001. In January 2009, Democrats ended the term limits for committee chairs in the House of Representatives.

1.2 Functions

House standing committees have two functions. Senate standing committees have the same two plus another. These functions are:

(1) To conduct the committee stage of the legislative process.

(2) To conduct investigations within the committee's policy area. This fulfils Congress's role of oversight of the executive branch, of which we shall learn more in Topic 5.H.

(3) **(In the Senate only)** To begin the confirmation process of numerous presidential appointments to both the executive and judicial branches of the federal government.

To fulfil these functions, standing committees hold **hearings** attended by **witnesses**. At the conclusion of hearings — which may last anything from a few hours to a day, to a week, or a month or more — votes will be taken to recommend action to the full chamber.

Make sure you get that right.

2 House Rules Committee

Officially this is one of the standing committees of the House, but it performs such a different function that it is better dealt with separately.

Nearly all bills pass through the House Rules Committee. It has the following functions:
- Timetables bills for consideration on the floor of the House.
- Deals with getting bills from the committee stage to the second reading.
- Prioritises the most important bills, giving them quick passage to the House floor.
- Gives a 'Rule' to each bill passing on to the floor for its second reading — the 'Rule' sets out the rules of debate by stating, for example, what, if any, amendments can be made to the bill at this stage.

A 'Rule' is best thought of as a kind of admission ticket to the House floor.

For these reasons, the House Rules Committee is potentially a very important committee.

3 Conference committees

Conference committees are required because of two important characteristics about the legislative process in the US Congress. First, both houses have equal power. Second, bills pass through both houses concurrently. As a consequence, there are two different versions of each bill — a House version and a Senate version. And by the time the bill has passed through each house, the two versions are likely to be very different. If after the third reading in each house the two versions of the bill are different, and if these differences cannot be sorted out informally, then a conference committee is set up.

'Ad hoc' = temporary.

Conference committees (whose members are referred to as 'conferees'):
- are ad hoc — set up to consider a particular bill and then disbanded
- contain members of both houses
- have one function — **to reconcile the differences between the two versions of the same bill**

When the conference committee has come up with an agreed version of the bill, this must be agreed to by a vote on the floor of each house. There has been a significant decline in the use of conference committees since 1995. Both parties when in the majority have often resorted to a more ad hoc, leadership-driven approach, where one chamber is simply asked to endorse the legislation passed by the other chamber in a system not dissimilar to what occurs in the UK parliament.

4 Select committees

Select committees are sometimes known as 'special committees' or 'investigative committees'. Nearly all are ad hoc, set up specially to investigate something in particular. Why have these select committees when, as we have already seen, the standing committees have an investigative function?

A select committee will be set up when the investigation either:
- does not fall within the policy area of one standing committee; or
- is likely to be so time-consuming that a standing committee would become tied up with it, thus preventing the standing committee from fulfilling its other functions.

Some examples of high-profile select committees from recent decades include:
- the Senate Select Committee on the Central Intelligence Agency
- the House Select Committee on political assassinations
- the Joint Select Committee on the Iran–Contra affair
- the Senate Select Committee on the Whitewater affair

F The legislative process

The legislative process in the US Congress is best thought of in seven stages:
(1) First reading
(2) Committee stage
(3) Timetabling
(4) Second reading
(5) Third reading
(6) Conference committee
(7) Presidential action

It is also important to remember the following points:
- **Both houses have equal power** when dealing with legislation.
- **Bills pass through the House and Senate concurrently.**
- A 'Congress' lasts for 2 years.
- Any bills not completed in one Congress must start the process again at the beginning in the next Congress.
- A huge number of bills — around 10–14,000 — are introduced during a Congress.
- Only a small proportion of these — around 400–450 — will be successfully passed into law — around 3–4%.
- The process is difficult and complicated.
- Supporters of a bill must win at every stage, whilst opponents have only to win at one stage to defeat a bill.
- There is little in the way of party discipline in Congress, which increases the difficulties.
- The president is unlikely to have his own party in control of both houses of Congress.
- It is even possible that the House and the Senate may be controlled by different parties, as between June 2001 and December 2002, with the Democrats controlling the Senate and the Republicans controlling the House.

But in reality there is about 20 months between one set of congressional elections and another to get bills through the process.

Table 5.4 gives you some idea as to the workload of recent Congresses. It is most important to note how few of the bills introduced are actually enacted.

	108th Congress 2003–2004	109th Congress 2005–06	110th Congress 2007–08
Bills introduced	10,669	13,072	14,042
Laws enacted	498 (5%)	395 (3%)	460 (3%)

Table 5.4 Workload of Congress, 2003–08

F *The legislative process*

1 First reading

- All 'money bills' must be introduced into the House first.
- There is no debate and no vote.
- It is just a formality.
- In the House, bills are placed in a hopper on the clerk's desk.
- In the Senate, the title is read out.
- Bills are then immediately sent on to the committee stage.

2 Committee stage

In the UK Parliament, the committee stage comes after the second reading.

- Bills are referred to one of the permanent, policy specialist standing committees (see E.1).
- It is important to note that the **committee stage comes before the second reading**.
- Committees have full power of amendment.
- Because of huge numbers of bills being referred to each committee, many bills are **pigeon-holed** — that is, merely put to one side and never considered.
- For a bill that is to be considered, a **hearing** is held with **witnesses** appearing before the committee.
- Hearings may be conducted either in the full committee or in **sub-committee**.
- Hearings can last from hours to days, weeks or even months, depending on the length of the bill and whether or not it is controversial.
- Once the hearings have been completed, the committee holds a **mark-up** session — making the changes it wishes — before **reporting out** the bill, effectively sending it on to its next stage.

The committee stage of a bill is of the utmost importance because:
- the committee members are regarded as the policy specialists so others look to the committee for a lead
- it is as far as most bills get
- committees have full power of amendment
- committees really do have life-and-death power over bills

3 Timetabling

Most textbooks do not give this as a separate stage, but I think it helps to make things clearer.

By the time Congress has been in session for a few months, a huge number of bills will be waiting to come to the floor of the House and the Senate for their second reading. Whilst there are dozens of committee and subcommittee rooms in each house, there is only one floor in each chamber. There develops something of a legislative traffic jam, with bills queuing for their turn on the House and Senate floors. Each house has a procedure for dealing with this potential problem.

The House of Representatives deals with this through **the House Rules Committee** (see E.2). The Senate deals with it through what are called **unanimous consent agreements**. These, in effect, are agreements between the Senate Majority and Minority Leaders (see D.2) on the order in which bills will be debated on the Senate floor.

A filibuster is the right of continuous debate. It can be ended by a 'closure' (or 'cloture') motion, which must be approved by three-fifths of the entire Senate (i.e. 60).

A recorded vote is sometimes called a 'roll-call vote'. In the Senate the clerk still 'calls the roll' of the 100 names alphabetically. In the House it is now a vote 'by electronic device'. Fifteen minutes is usually allowed for members to cast their votes.

Members are called 'conferees'.

4 Second reading

- The first opportunity for most members to debate the bill.
- In the House, most bills are debated in the **Committee of the Whole House**, allowing for different rules of debate.
- In the Senate, bills can be subject to **filibustering**.
- In both houses, further amendments can usually be made.
- Votes will be taken on amendments — simple majorities required to pass.
- At the end of the debate, a vote will be taken on the bill.
- The vote will be either a **voice vote** (for non-controversial bills) or a **recorded vote**, in which a record of each member's vote is made.
- A simple majority is required to pass the bill.

5 Third reading

- A final opportunity to debate the bill.
- If substantial amendments were made at the second reading, the third reading is likely to occur some weeks or months after the second reading and require another substantive debate.
- If few amendments were made at the second reading, or these amendments were approved by large majorities, the third reading may follow on almost immediately after the second reading and be a very brief debate.
- At the end of the debate, another vote will be taken.

6 Conference committee

- An optional stage.
- Members are drawn from both houses.
- If the House version and the Senate version of the bill are the same, there is no need for a conference committee.
- If differences in the two versions of the bill can be sorted out amicably between the two houses, there is no need for a conference committee.
- If there are **substantial differences** between the two versions of the bill and these **cannot be sorted out amicably**, then a conference committee may be used (see E.3).

7 Presidential action

A bill can be passed to the president once the House and Senate have agreed on a single version of the bill.

The president always has **three options**:

(1) **To sign the bill into law:** this he will do to bills he fully supports, wants to be associated with and take credit for; he must sign the bill within ten congressional working days of receiving it.

(2) **To leave the bill on his desk:** this he will do to bills he only partly supports, those he takes no position on at all, or those he would wish to veto but has decided not to. These bills will become law without his signature within ten congressional working days.

President George W. Bush used no vetoes during his first term and only 11 in his second term.

President George W. Bush used only one pocket veto during his entire 8 years, when he pocket-vetoed a defence authorisation bill in December 2007.

During the brief time that President Clinton had the power, he used it on 11 bills.

(3) **To veto the bill:** this he will do to bills he clearly opposes. He must veto the bill within ten congressional working days of receiving it by sending it back to its house of origin with a note explaining his objections. To override the veto, the bill must be passed by a two-thirds majority in both houses. This is very difficult to achieve. Congress managed to override only two of Bill Clinton's 36 regular vetoes in 8 years. However, they overrode four of George W. Bush's 11 regular vetoes in his 8 years. (For more detail on presidential vetoes, see Topic 6.A.4.)

At the end of a congressional session, the president has a **fourth option**:

(4) **To pocket-veto the bill:** if, whilst the bill is awaiting the president's action, the congressional session ends, the bill is lost. This is called a **pocket veto** and it cannot be overridden by Congress.

For about a year during the Clinton presidency, the President had a **fifth option — the line-item veto**. This allowed him to sign parts of a bill into law whilst vetoing other parts to do with spending. But in 1998, the Supreme Court declared the power unconstitutional.

G Voting in Congress

House and Senate members are called upon to cast a large number of votes each year — in 2008, 690 recorded votes in the House and 215 in the Senate. They might be voting on budgets, amendments to bills, second or third readings, bills from conference committees, constitutional amendments, or in the Senate on treaties or appointments made by the president. And they will probably be rushing to the floor to cast their vote, having just broken off a committee hearing or a meeting with constituents or staff.

What factors make them vote as they do? In the UK House of Commons, the answer would be quite simple — party. But in the US Congress, political parties are only one of a number of factors that determine the way members vote.

One should consider six important determinants of voting:
(1) Political party
(2) Constituents
(3) The administration
(4) Pressure groups
(5) Colleagues and staff
(6) Personal beliefs

The relative importance of these determinants will vary from one politician to another and from one vote to another.

1 *Political party*

Political party is one of a number of determinants of voting in Congress. For some members, on some issues, it may be the most important determinant. But it is by no means the all-important determinant that it is for MPs in the UK House of Commons.

There are five important reasons for this difference:

(1) Political parties in the USA are far less centralised and ideologically cohesive than their UK counterparts.

(2) US political parties do not have the 'sticks' and 'carrots' that their UK counterparts have as incentives to party unity — 'sticks' such as threats of de-selection or 'carrots' such as much sought-after jobs in the executive branch.

(3) Constituents control the selection of candidates — through congressional primaries — so House and Senate members have to be far more watchful of constituents' views than of the party view.

(4) House members are subject to elections every 2 years, increasing their reliance on the views of their constituents.

(5) The executive branch does not depend for its existence on getting its policies through the legislature, as it does in the UK.

It is also important to realise what political commentators mean in the USA by a **party vote** in the legislature. In the UK House of Commons, a party vote would mean all the MPs on the government side of the House voting against all the MPs on the opposition side. A huge number of votes in the UK House of Commons would fit that description. But in the US Congress, when we talk of a party vote, we mean one in which the majority of one party votes against the majority of the other party.

Take the example of a vote in the House of Representatives, on the 9/11 Recommendations Implementation bill on 8 October 2004:

● It passed by 282 to 134.
● Republicans voted 213 yes; 8 no.
● Democrats voted 69 yes; 125 no.
● The Independent House member voted 'no'.
● The majority of Republicans voted 'yes'.
● The majority of Democrats voted 'no'.

Therefore this would classify as a 'party vote', despite the fact that 77 members (8 Republicans and 69 Democrats) broke with their party majorities.

Year	House	Senate
1999	47%	63%
2000	43%	49%
2001	55%	40%
2002	43%	45%
2003	52%	67%
2004	47%	52%
2005	49%	63%
2006	55%	57%
2007	62%	60%
2008	53%	52%

Table 5.5 Party votes as a percentage of all recorded votes, 1999–2008

Despite this very low threshold for qualifying as a 'party vote', in recent years only around 50–60% of votes in each chamber have been party votes, as Table 5.5 shows.

A more typical vote in the House or the Senate is one in which the majority of members of both parties vote the same way.

Take, for example, a vote in the House, on 7 December 2004, on the Intelligence Reform and Terrorism Prevention bill:

● It passed by 336–75.
● Republicans voted 152–67.
● Democrats voted 183–8.
● Independent voted 1–0.

2 Constituents

Why do House and Senate members place the views of their constituents so highly in their voting priorities?

There are four reasons to consider:

(1) The Constitution states that House and Senate members must be residents of the state they represent, so this gives them a good understanding of what 'the folks back home' are saying.

(2) A number of states go further by insisting that House members reside in the actual district (constituency) they represent.

(3) Many House and Senate members will have been born and educated, lived and worked in the state/district they now represent.

(4) House members are especially careful about constituents' views because they have to face election every 2 years.

This is known as the 'locality rule'.

How do House and Senate members find out what their constituents want whilst they are working in Washington DC? There are various methods, which include:

- visits from constituents
- phone calls, letters, faxes and e-mails from constituents
- keeping in constant touch with their offices back in the state/district
- reading the newspapers published in their state/district

But they will also discover what their constituents want by making frequent visits back to their state/district. The frequency will depend on how far this is from Washington DC. Once back in their state/district, House and Senate members will:

- hold party meetings
- hold 'town hall' meetings
- conduct 'surgeries' with individual constituents
- make visits around the state/district
- appear on local radio phone-in programmes
- be interviewed by representatives of the local media
- address various groups such as chambers of commerce, professional groups, Round Table lunches etc.
- visit local schools, hospitals and businesses

All these will help them keep in touch with the views of their constituents.

However, when it comes to voting, three further factors must be remembered:

(1) Except on some exceptional issues, local opinion on any given issue is likely to be divided, with some in favour and some against.

(2) Through constituency mail and visits, the House/Senate member is more likely to hear from the discontented than the contented.

(3) A member of Congress is meant to be more than just a mere 'delegate' of their constituents and may need to balance other factors, as well as the national good, against what is perceived as being merely locally popular.

This is very important. Candidates too often talk of constituency interest as if on all issues everyone in the state or district thinks the same way. Would that it were that simple!

3 The administration

The term 'administration' means members of the executive branch. Remember that much of the legislation being voted on in Congress will have been initiated by the president or members of his administration. Cabinet members — the heads of the 15 executive departments — will have a keen interest in the passage of legislation affecting their policy areas. So members of the administration — from the departments and agencies, as well as the White House itself — will keep in contact with members of Congress and will attempt to persuade them to cast their votes in certain ways. They will do this through phone calls as well as visits. They will talk with members of the relevant committees, with staff members working in the Washington offices of House and Senate members.

Often, the White House itself will get involved. This will be done either by the Congressional Liaison Office or directly by the president himself.

Such persuasion will need to be regular and bipartisan. It is important that members of Congress are approached regularly and not only just before an important vote is coming up. It is also important that those from departments and the White House are willing to do favours in return, offering a two-way street of mutual cooperation. And all this will need to be done with members from both parties. For an administration to talk only with members of their party is usually a recipe for disaster. Things tend to happen in Congress when they are supported by a bipartisan coalition.

'Bipartisan' = of two parties.

4 *Pressure groups*

Pressure groups will use a number of different ways to try to influence the way House and Senate members cast their votes. These include contacts with members and staff in Congress, as well as attempts to generate public support favourable to their position. They will make visits and phone calls, provide evidence to support their position, organise rallies, demonstrations and petition drives both in Washington and around the country, as well as engage in significant fundraising. Money raised will be used to fund politicians who support their cause and to seek to defeat those who do not. Certain policy areas have seen significant pressure group activity, including the environment, abortion, gun control, health care, welfare reform and international trade (see Topic 4).

5 *Colleagues and staff*

Remember that members of Congress have to cast literally hundreds of votes every year. No politician can know all the details of all these votes. They will therefore tend to rely on other people for help in how they might vote.

Don't underestimate the importance of senior staff. I have been with a House member walking to the House to vote, who turned to a staff member and said: 'How am I voting on this one?'

Before going to the floor to vote, many House and Senate members will have checked with:

- their senior legislative staff
- fellow members of their own party who share their philosophy and views, especially senior, respected members who may become almost their mentors
- members from the same state and, in the House, members from neighbouring districts

- members of the relevant standing committee who considered the legislation at the committee stage

6 *Personal beliefs*

On certain votes, a House or Senate member may vote in a certain way because of their own personal beliefs. Issues upon which this factor is likely to be uppermost will be votes regarding such matters as abortion, capital punishment, tax increases (or tax cuts), federal subsidies or defence spending. There are, for example, members of Congress who, because of their own personal beliefs, will never vote for federal subsidies to any industry or group, even if that means going against a party line, the administration's views or their own constituents.

H Oversight of the executive branch

Congress not only has the function of passing legislation but also of oversight of the executive branch. This function is not specially granted by the Constitution but is an implied power. Members of Congress have to know what is going on in order to make the laws, as well as see how the laws they have passed are working.

It is important to remember when dealing with Congress's oversight function that the executive is physically separated from the legislature. Unlike in the UK, members of the executive are not — cannot be — serving members of the legislature. Senators Barack Obama and Joe Biden both had to resign from the Senate in order to become, respectively, president and vice-president in January 2009. So did Senators Hillary Clinton and Ken Salazar and Representative Hilda Solis in order to join the Obama cabinet. That would, of course, not be the case in the UK. But the important consequence of this fact is that there cannot be anything resembling Question Time in the US Congress, for the simple reason that executive branch members are not physically present.

As a result of that, most oversight of the executive branch occurs not in the chambers of the House or the Senate, but in the committee rooms of Congress — mainly the standing committees. It is here that executive branch members — though not usually the president — appear on a regular basis to answer detailed policy questions from committee members. And because standing committee members are themselves policy specialists, questioning is often detailed and thorough.

However, this leads to an important question regarding Congress's effectiveness in its oversight function. Some suggest that congressional oversight works well only when Congress and the president are controlled by different parties —

at times of divided government. At times of united government — such as during the middle 4 years of George W. Bush's presidency (2003–06) — there is much evidence that Congress operates more like a lapdog than a watchdog. An example of this would be the Republican Congress's feeble oversight of the war in Iraq between 2003 and 2006. The trouble is that during times of divided government, congressional oversight often degenerates into political point-scoring and attempts to embarrass, rather than investigate, the administration. An example of this would be Democrats' attempt to embarrass President Bush during the last 2 years of his administration, 2007–08.

Questions

1 What is the term used about Congress which means that it is made up of two chambers?

2 **(a)** How many members are in the House of Representatives? **(b)** How are they distributed amongst the states? **(c)** What length terms do they serve? **(d)** What are the three constitutional requirements to be a House member?

3 **(a)** How many members are in the Senate? **(b)** How are they distributed amongst the states? **(c)** What length terms do they serve? **(d)** What are the three constitutional requirements to be a senator?

4 **(a)** What are the three exclusive powers of the House? **(b)** What are the four exclusive powers of the Senate?

5 What are the five joint powers of both houses?

6 Give four reasons why the Senate is often thought of as being more prestigious and powerful than the House.

7 What are the powers of the Speaker of the House of Representatives?

8 What is the 'seniority rule'?

9 What are the functions of congressional standing committees?

10 What are the functions of the House Rules Committee?

11 What do conference committees do?

12 Why is the committee stage of the legislative process so important?

13 What options are open to the president when a bill is passed to him?

14 How can Congress override a presidential veto?

15 What six factors are said to influence the way members of Congress vote?

16 Why is congressional oversight of the executive done mostly in committee rather than in the actual House and Senate chambers?

There are two popular misconceptions about the US presidency. The first is that it is purely a one-man band. Although 'the president' might be thought of as such, 'the presidency' is much more like an orchestra, and a large one at that, made up of literally hundreds of people. The second misconception is that the president is hugely powerful — 'the most powerful person in the world' is a much-used phrase. Again, although there may be a grain of truth in this, students of US politics need to discover that the office of the US president is often very limited and, for its occupant, hugely frustrating. The presidency is therefore something of a paradox.

Note that a president's term of office begins the year after the election. The election is in November, but the new president does not take over until the following January.

President	Party	Dates
John Kennedy	Democrat	1961–63
Lyndon Johnson	Democrat	1963–69
Richard Nixon	Republican	1969–74
Gerald Ford	Republican	1974–77
Jimmy Carter	Democrat	1977–81
Ronald Reagan	Republican	1981–89
George H.W. Bush	Republican	1989–93
Bill Clinton	Democrat	1993–2001
George W. Bush	Republican	2001–09
Barack Obama	Democrat	2009–

Table 6.1 American presidents since 1961

The topic is divided into six major headings:

A The powers of the president

B The federal bureaucracy

C The cabinet

D The Executive Office of the President

E Relations with Congress

F Limits on presidential power

A The powers of the president

The powers of the president are his tasks, functions or duties. They are laid out in Article II of the Constitution. Essentially, they are the same for every president. These powers have been held by George Washington and Barack Obama, and all the 41 presidents in between.

The president has the following powers:
- To propose legislation to Congress.
- To submit the annual budget to Congress.
- To sign legislation passed by Congress.
- To veto legislation passed by Congress.
- To act as chief executive.
- To nominate executive branch officials.
- To nominate judges.
- To act as commander-in-chief.
- To negotiate treaties.
- To pardon felons.

1   *Propose legislation*

The phrase comes from Article II, Section 3: 'He shall from time to time give to the Congress information of the state of the Union.'

The president proposes legislation to Congress in a number of ways — most obviously through the annual **State of the Union Address**, when he addresses a joint session of Congress. This occurs each January, and it gives the president the chance to set out a legislative agenda for the coming year. But the president can propose legislation at any time by, for example, calling a press conference or making an announcement at some public event.

Some examples of presidential initiatives by President Clinton were:
- health-care reform
- welfare reform
- anti-crime legislation
- gun control legislation
- reform of the social security system

2   *Submit the annual budget*

The annual federal budget is drawn up for the president by the Office of Management and Budget (see section D.4). The president then submits it to Congress. This is followed by a lengthy bargaining process between the president and Congress — especially lengthy if the president and Congress are controlled by different political parties.

3   *Sign legislation*

Once bills have passed through a lengthy and complicated process in Congress (see Topic 5.F), they land on the president's desk. He has a number of options, but the most likely is that of signing the bill into law. He will do this to bills for which he wishes to take some credit. Elaborate bill-signing ceremonies are often held, attended by House and Senate members who have been particularly supportive, as well as interested parties who will be affected by the new legislation.

4 Veto legislation

As well as signing bills into law, the president has the option of vetoing them. The **regular veto** is a much-used presidential weapon. Even the threat of it can be an important bargaining tool. Table 6.2 shows the use of the veto by recent presidents. Altogether, from George Washington through to the end of the presidency of George W. Bush, presidents have used under 1,500 regular vetoes, of which Congress have overridden just 110 (7%). George W. Bush's success rate of just below 64% was the third lowest of any president. Only Franklin Pierce (1853–57) and Andrew Johnson (1865–69) scored lower.

President	Regular vetoes used	Vetoes overridden	President's success rate (%)
John Kennedy	12	0	100
Lyndon Johnson	16	0	100
Richard Nixon	26	7	73
Gerald Ford	48	12	75
Jimmy Carter	13	2	85
Ronald Reagan	39	9	77
George H.W. Bush	29	1	98
Bill Clinton	36	2	95
George W. Bush	11	4	64

Table 6.2 Regular vetoes and overrides, 1961–2008

To veto a bill, the president must:
- **veto the whole bill**, not just parts of it
- return the bill to the house which first considered it, within ten working days
- include a note explaining any objections

> This note is called the 'veto message'.

It is then up to Congress to decide what to do. Congress may decide to:
- do nothing — conceding that the president has won and the bill will not become law
- attempt to override the president's veto

> It is important to say 'a two-thirds majority in both houses'. To say 'a two-thirds majority in Congress' is at best misleading.

> They will judge this by looking at the 'final passage' vote in each house to see how small or large the majority was.

If Congress decides to attempt to override the president's veto then the bill must be given a **two-thirds** majority vote **in both houses of Congress**. But as we now know, this is exceedingly difficult to achieve. If Congress knows it cannot override the president's veto, it may well have given concessions to him whilst the bill was going through the legislative process. Furthermore, presidents will often choose not to veto bills if they know that Congress will override them. To have a veto overridden by Congress is politically damaging, especially if — as in the case of Jimmy Carter — it is inflicted by a Congress controlled by the president's own party.

Table 6.3 gives three examples of some of George W. Bush's regular vetoes. In the first, Congress admits defeat and doesn't even try to override the President's veto. The veto is sustained. In the second, the House votes to override the veto but fails to achieve the required two-thirds majority. With 412 House members voting, 275 votes were required to override the veto. The House vote fell 12 votes short of that. The veto was sustained. In the third, both houses achieve a two-thirds majority and the President's veto was overridden — the bill became law.

Bill	Final House vote	Final Senate vote	Vetoed by president	House vote to override veto	Senate vote to override veto	Result
Stem Cell Research	247–176	63–34	20/6/2007	–	–	Sustained
Child's Health Insurance	265–142	64–30	12/12/2007	260–152	–	Sustained
Food Conservation/ Energy	**306–110**	**77–15**	**18/6/2008**	**317–109**	**80–14**	**Overridden**

Table 6.3 George W. Bush's regular vetoes: selected examples

The president may also have the power of **pocket veto** at his disposal. But this can be used only after a session of Congress has adjourned. When Congress is in session, a bill becomes law after ten working days if the president neither signs nor vetoes it. But when Congress has adjourned and the president does not sign the bill, the bill is lost. This is called a pocket veto. Because Congress is no longer in session, pocket vetoes cannot be overridden. President Clinton used only one pocket veto during his 8 years — in December 2000, when he pocket-vetoed a consumer bankruptcy overhaul bill. President Reagan used 39 pocket vetoes during his 8 years in office and President George H.W. Bush used 17 during his 4 years. George W. Bush used only one pocket veto in his 8 years in office.

5 *Act as chief executive*

The opening words of Article II of the Constitution state that: 'The executive power shall be vested in a president of the United States of America.' This makes the president the chief executive, in charge of running the executive branch of the federal government. This is a huge job and much of the day-to-day running is delegated to those who run the principal departments and agencies of the federal government (see section B of this topic).

6 *Nominate executive branch officials*

The State Department is the US equivalent of the UK's Foreign Office.

The president is given the power to nominate hundreds of officials to the executive branch of the federal government. The most important of these are the heads of the 15 executive departments such as State, Treasury and Agriculture. At the beginning of his presidency, Barack Obama nominated Hillary Clinton to be Secretary of State, Arne Duncan to be Secretary of Education and Tom Vilsack to be Secretary of Agriculture. All of these, of course, had to be confirmed by the Senate by simple majority vote. Robert Gates was kept on as Secretary of Defense from the George W. Bush administration and so did not need to be reconfirmed, having been confirmed in that post back in December 2006 (see Table 6.4).

Nominee	Post	Year appointed	Senate vote
Hillary Clinton	Secretary of State	2009	94–2
Robert Gates	Secretary of Defense	2006	95–2[†]
Timothy Geithner	Secretary of the Treasury	2009	60–34
Tom Vilsack	Secretary of Agriculture	2009	Voice vote
Ken Salazar	Secretary of the Interior	2009	Voice vote
Eric Holder	Attorney General	2009	75–21
Gary Locke	Secretary of Commerce	2009	Voice vote
Hilda Solis	Secretary of Labor	2009	80–17
Kathleen Sebelius	Secretary of Health and Human Services	2009	65–31
Arne Duncan	Secretary of Education	2009	Voice vote
Shaun Donovan	Secretary of Housing and Urban Development	2009	Voice vote
Ray LaHood	Secretary of Transportation	2009	Voice vote
Steven Chu	Secretary of Energy	2009	Voice vote
Eric Shinseki	Secretary of Veterans' Affairs	2009	Voice vote
Janet Napolitano	Secretary of Homeland Security	2009	Voice vote

The Attorney General heads the Justice Department.

[†] Confirmed December 2006

Table 6.4 Barack Obama's cabinet nominees and confirmation votes, 2009

7 *Nominate federal judges*

Again, this involves the president in making hundreds of appointments. Not only must he fill up vacancies on the Supreme Court, he must also do this for the trial and appeal courts of the federal government. All judicial appointments are for life and therefore assume a special importance. And the most important are those to the Supreme Court (see Topic 8.A). During his 8 years in office, President George W. Bush appointed two members to the Supreme Court, John Roberts as Chief Justice (2005) and Samuel Alito as an associate justice (2006). At the time of writing, there are still appointees of presidents Ford (1974–77) and Reagan (1981–89) on the Supreme Court.

8 *Act as commander-in-chief*

This was a particularly significant power for the presidents in office between the 1940s and the early 1990s — from Franklin Roosevelt to George H.W. Bush.

The events of 11
September 2001
clearly showed that.

With the USA fighting in the Second World War and then taking the lead for the West in the Cold War, the president's commander-in-chief role was highly significant during a period that also saw the Korean War, the Vietnam War and the Gulf War, as well as the wars in Iraq and Afghanistan during the presidency of George W. Bush — to name only the principal conflicts. Arguably, in the post-Cold War era, this power is less to the fore. But crises will still occur and the power is potentially an important one. Again, the president is checked by Congress's 'power of the purse': its power to declare war and to conduct investigations.

9 *Negotiate treaties*

The president's seal of office shows an eagle clutching a bundle of arrows in one claw, symbolising the commander-in-chief role, and an olive branch in the other to symbolise his peace-making role. Modern-day presidents have used this power to negotiate such treaties as the Panama Canal Treaty (Jimmy Carter), the Strategic Arms Reduction Treaty (Ronald Reagan) and the Chemical Weapons Ban (George Bush).

Again, the president's power is checked by the Senate's power to ratify treaties. Table 6.5 shows that during the twentieth century, the Senate rejected treaties negotiated by the president on seven occasions. The 1999 occasion was the only one in which the treaty failed to gain even a simple majority, let alone the two-thirds majority required for ratification.

Date	President	Treaty	Senate vote (yes–no)
19 March 1920	Woodrow Wilson	Treaty of Versailles	49–35
18 January 1927	Calvin Coolidge	Commercial rights	50–34
14 March 1934	Franklin Roosevelt	St Lawrence Seaway	46–42
29 January 1935	Franklin Roosevelt	World Court	52–36
26 March 1960	Dwight Eisenhower	Law of Sea Convention	49–30
8 March 1983	Ronald Reagan	Montreal Protocol	50–42
13 October 1999	Bill Clinton	Comprehensive Test Ban	48–51

Table 6.5 Senate rejection of treaties since 1920

10 *Pardon*

Presidents possess the power of pardon. Mostly used in uncontroversial cases, this power has occasionally been used in high-profile and controversial ones. The most notable was President Ford's 1974 pardon of former President Richard Nixon. President George H.W. Bush caused controversy with his 1992 pardon of former Defense Secretary Caspar Weinberger, as did President Clinton when he issued 140 pardons on his last day in office in January 2001. President George W. Bush used the power sparingly, issuing only 189 in 8 years.

B The federal bureaucracy

1 Twentieth-century expansion

Executive departments are also called 'cabinet departments' because their heads make up the president's cabinet.

With the expansion of the federal government (see Topic 1.E.4), the federal bureaucracy has grown hugely. Under George Washington, there were just three **executive departments** — State, War (later renamed Defense) and Treasury. By the time Theodore Roosevelt became president at the beginning of the twentieth century, a further three had been added — Interior, Justice and Agriculture. But that century saw another nine departments added. These included such areas as Health, Housing and Urban Development, Transportation and Energy. By 2005, there were 15 executive departments (see Table 6.6).

Executive department	Created
State	1789
Treasury	1789
Defense	1949
Justice	1870
Interior	1849
Agriculture	1889
Commerce	1903
Labor	1903
Health and Human Services	1953
Housing and Urban Development	1965
Transportation	1966
Energy	1977
Education	1979
Veterans' Affairs	1989
Homeland Security	2002

Table 6.6 Executive departments and dates created

2 The size and scale of today's bureaucracy

But that is not all. Add to that the huge number of **executive agencies** and **regulatory commissions**. Today these number in the region of 60 and include such bodies as the National Aeronautics and Space Administration (NASA), the Central Intelligence Agency (CIA), the Environmental Protection Agency (EPA) and the Federal Election Commission (FEC).

Together, the departments, agencies and commissions have some 3 million civilian employees. (Add another 2 million for the military.) And, needless to say, these 3 million civil servants do not all work in Washington DC. The federal bureaucracy is spread throughout the entire USA. There are **federal government** offices in every good-sized US city. In 1995, it was the federal government building in Oklahoma City that was the target of a major act of terrorism.

This is why the president has such a difficult job running the federal bureaucracy. It is big and it is spread across 4,500 km and four time zones. And don't forget also that many federal government programmes are dependent upon implementation by **state governments**. Former President Jimmy Carter commented: 'Before I became president, I was warned that dealing with the federal bureaucracy would be one of the worst problems I would have to face. It has been even worse than I had anticipated.'

C The cabinet

1 Definition and membership

Another 'scholarly' quotation for your essays.

The president's cabinet is not mentioned in the Constitution. According to presidential scholar Richard Fenno, it is **'institutionalised by usage alone'**. In other words, 'it's used because it's used'. The cabinet is an **advice-giving group** selected by the president to aid him in making decisions, membership of which is determined both by tradition and presidential discretion. By tradition, it is made up of the heads of the 15 executive departments. By presidential discretion, others can be given 'cabinet rank'. These might include the US ambassador to the United Nations and the US trade representative.

2 Cabinet recruitment

You can use the terms 'cabinet members' or 'cabinet officers' but not 'cabinet ministers'.

Unlike an incoming British prime minister, a newly elected US president such as Barack Obama does not have a 'shadow cabinet' ready and waiting to form the new administration. And, unlike in the British parliamentary system, where cabinet members are drawn from the legislature, members of the US president's cabinet cannot be currently serving members of Congress. Between 1961 and 2009, fewer than one in five cabinet officers had any previous experience in Congress. However, amongst Barack Obama's original 15 heads of departments in 2009, four had congressional experience, of which three were serving members of Congress who had to resign their seats.

Members of the president's cabinet will, therefore, come from a very diverse background. These are likely to include:
- Congress, but these must be either former members or those willing to resign their seats (e.g. former House member Ray LaHood as Secretary of Transportation in the new cabinet of Barack Obama, who had just retired from the House in 2008)

- state governors (e.g. Governor Janet Napolitano of Arizona as Secretary of Homeland Security in 2009)
- city mayors (e.g. Clinton's Secretary of Transportation, Federico Peña, had been Mayor of Denver)
- academics (e.g. Steven Chu, Barack Obama's Secretary of Energy, has been a professor of physics at Stanford University)

It is also highly likely that cabinet members will be policy specialists. Again, here are three such examples from the initial cabinet of President Barack Obama:

- Timothy Geithner (Treasury) — President of the Federal Reserve Bank of New York, 2003–09
- Arne Duncan (Education) — CEO of Chicago Public (i.e. state) Schools, 2001–09
- Shaun Donovan (Housing and Urban Development) — New York City Housing Commissioner, 2004–09

Because most cabinet members are policy specialists, there are no such things in US politics as 'cabinet reshuffles', those great bonanzas of speculation that exist in UK politics. Over the last 48 years (1961–2008), only 11 cabinet officers have ever headed more than one department. Some recent examples are given in Table 6.7.

Cabinet officer	Departments headed	President	Years
James Baker	Treasury State	Reagan George H.W. Bush	1985–88 1989–92
Elizabeth Dole	Transportation Labor	Reagan George H.W. Bush	1983–87 1989–91
Federico Peña	Transportation Energy	Clinton Clinton	1993–97 1997–98
Norman Mineta	Commerce Transportation	Clinton George W. Bush	2000–01 2001–06

Table 6.7 Cabinet officers who have headed more than one department: selected examples

Presidents also like to balance their cabinet in terms of geographic region, race, gender, ideology and age. Incoming President Clinton in 1993 even went so far as to talk about having a cabinet that 'looked like America'. President Barack Obama included in his first cabinet:

- a Lebanese-American (Ray LaHood)
- an African-American (Eric Holder)
- a Chinese-American (Steven Chu)
- two Japanese-Americans (Eric Shinseki and Gary Locke)
- two Hispanics (Hilda Solis and Ken Salazar)

This made Obama's cabinet the most ethnically diverse ever appointed.

All cabinet appointments have to be confirmed by a simple majority vote of the Senate. The last time the Senate rejected a president's cabinet appointee was in 1989, when they rejected John Tower, George Bush's nominee to head the Defense Department. In 2009, Hillary Clinton was confirmed as Secretary of State by 94 votes to 2 (see Table 6.4 for details).

3 *Cabinet meetings*

Meetings of the president with the full cabinet tend to get a pretty bad press. Many who have attended them describe them as boring and a waste of time. Indeed, some presidents have held very few. Most presidents have held cabinet meetings only about once a month. Clinton managed only two or three a year, whilst at the other extreme both Presidents Carter and Reagan held 36 meetings in their first year in office. The number of meetings tends to decline as the administration wears on. There are three principal reasons for this:

(1) Some of the functions of the cabinet are no longer applicable.

(2) The president has increasing calls on his time, not least when he has to run for re-election. Jimmy Carter managed only six cabinet meetings in his final year in office.

(3) Presidents tend to become disillusioned with their cabinet officers, often believing them to be disloyal. In the words of Nixon White House aide John Ehrlichman, the cabinet go off and 'marry the natives'.

> 'The natives' being the bureaucrats in their own departments.

And cabinet meetings have had some fairly poor reviews. Consider the following selection:

> Some 'original' quotations. Good essay material!

- 'The President listened to the group with thinly disguised impatience.' (J. Edward Day, Kennedy cabinet member)
- 'I always went to cabinet meetings thinking, "I wonder how soon I can get away from this so I can get on with all the work I've got to do." And I think most of my colleagues had the same idea.' (A Johnson cabinet member)
- 'Nothing of substance was discussed. There was no disagreement because there was nothing to disagree about. Things over which one might have disagreed were not discussed.' (Elliot Richardson, a Nixon cabinet member)
- 'Carter cabinet meetings were almost useless. The discussions were desultory. There was no coherent theme to them, and after a while they were held less and less frequently.' (Zbigniew Brzezinski, National Security Advisor to President Carter)
- 'Very often they were a waste of time. You could get very bored.' (A member of President George H.W. Bush's cabinet)

Nonetheless, cabinet meetings can perform useful functions, both for the president and for cabinet members. They can enable the president to:

- engender team spirit — especially at the beginning of his administration
- look collegial and consultative
- give information to all cabinet members
- glean information from cabinet members — find out what's going on in each department
- debate policies
- present 'big picture' items such as the budget, tours, campaigns, initiatives
- check up on legislation going through Congress in which he has an interest
- see cabinet members he wouldn't otherwise see

> This was the main function of George W. Bush's cabinet meetings.
>
> Can you imagine a British cabinet minister claiming this as a function of meetings at Number 10? Hardly!

For cabinet members themselves, cabinet meetings serve:

- as get-to-know-you sessions — especially at the beginning of an administration when a number of cabinet colleagues may be total strangers
- to sort out inter-departmental disputes

- as a means of catching other members (before and/or after the meetings)
- as an opportunity to see the president — whom many of them wouldn't otherwise see
- to gain them prestige back at their department, with first-hand news of what the president wants

Not all cabinet members have rubbished the meetings. Consider the following:
- 'Cabinet meetings were often vigorous, such as the one on the pros and cons of building the Russian oil pipeline. It was quite a shouting match.' (Frank Carlucci, Defense Secretary to President Reagan)
- 'At the meeting prior to the Malta Summit [with Soviet President Gorbachev in December 1989], for example, the President engaged the cabinet in a very significant discussion of foreign policy. I think the cabinet valued the opportunity to present their views directly and candidly. It allowed the President to broaden his consultations.' (Michael Jackson, member of President George H.W. Bush's Office of Cabinet Affairs)

4 Cabinet councils

One of the main problems associated with full cabinet meetings is that because members are likely to be policy specialists, many will find policy-specific agenda items — other than those in their area — of no interest at all. To get round this problem, some recent presidents have developed a series of more policy-specific cabinet councils. These existed during the presidencies of Ronald Reagan, George Bush and George W. Bush and have been continued in the administration of Barack Obama. There are currently three in existence in the Obama administration:
- The Economic Policy Council
- The Domestic Policy Council
- The National Security Council

As a result, full cabinet meetings are held less frequently and tend to be reserved for 'team talks' by the president at key moments in the political calendar — just before a State of the Union address, a budget proposal, a foreign tour, an election cycle.

5 Relations with the Executive Office of the President

It must be remembered that the principal job of cabinet officers is not to act as presidential advisors. There are good reasons why not:
- They have huge departments to run.
- They are not based in the White House.
- They have loyalties other than those to the president.

The last reason often leads to accusations of disloyalty from those whose principal function it is to act as 'all the president's men', i.e. the members of the Executive Office of the President (EXOP), which includes the White House staff (see section D). For whilst members of EXOP serve only the president, cabinet

This is sometimes abbreviated to EOP.

These three —
Congress, the
bureaucracy, pressure
groups — are
sometimes referred to
as 'the iron triangle'.

members must bear in mind the wishes of Congress (whose votes decide their departmental budgets), their own departmental bureaucracy, as well as interest groups which have important links with their department. Unlike the Cabinet, members of EXOP enjoy close proximity and access to the president.

Presidential scholar Richard Neustadt has written: '[An incoming president] must prepare the cabinet members against the shocking discovery that most of them are not the principal advisors to the president, are not going to be, and never will be, not since the White House staff has come into mature existence.'

In essays, it is very
important to make
clear the distinction
between the cabinet
as *individuals* and the
cabinet as a *collectivity*.

6   *The cabinet: important or unimportant?*

How important is the cabinet? Individually very important, though some far more than others. They run huge executive departments and spend vast budgets. But collectively, the cabinet can never be that important. There are six main reasons for this:

(1) Article II of the Constitution states that 'all executive power shall be vested in a president'.

(2) There is no doctrine of collective responsibility.

(3) The president is not 'first among equals' — he is just 'first'. As Anthony King has stated: 'He doesn't sum up at the end of the meeting; he *is* the meeting.'

(4) Cabinet officers are not his political rivals; they are not about to become president.

(5) They have a problem of divided loyalty as well as a lack of proximity and access to the president.

(6) The president has EXOP, which is important in helping and advising him to achieve his goals.

'The very nature of the cabinet — a body with no constitutional standing, members with no independent political base of their own and no requirement that the president seeks or follows their advice — helps contribute to its lack of influence as a collective body.' (Professor Michael Genovese)

D The Executive Office of the President

Named after its chair,
Dr Louis Brownlow.

1   *Definition and membership*

The Executive Office of the President is an umbrella term for an organisation that consists of the top presidential staff agencies that provide help, advice, coordination and administrative support for the president.

Created in 1939, after the **Brownlow Committee** reported that **'the president needs help'**, EXOP has grown to include around a dozen or so offices. The most important ones are:
● the White House Office

- the National Security Council
- the Office of Management and Budget

Why did presidents from the mid-twentieth century 'need help' in running the federal government? There were three main reasons:
- The huge increase in the size and scale of the federal government caused by nineteenth-century westward expansion and industrialisation.
- The 'New Deal' programme introduced by FDR to help cure the effects of the Depression.
- The USA's newly found role as a world power.

2 The White House Office

The White House Office includes the president's most trusted and closest aides and advisors, such as:
- Press Secretary
- Chief of Staff
- Assistant to the President for Legislative Affairs

The principal function of those who work in the White House Office is to provide advice and administrative support for the president on a daily basis. This will involve:
- policy advice
- personnel management
- crisis management
- liaison with the federal bureaucracy
- liaison with Congress
- running the White House
- deciding and executing the president's daily schedule
- acting as 'lightning conductors' for the president
- ensuring an orderly decision-making process for the president

Members of the White House staff are meant to act not as policy-makers, but as **'honest brokers'**. They are not meant to be always in the media spotlight, but to have something of a **'passion for anonymity'**. As then White House Chief of Staff Dick Cheney stated of his relationship with President Ford: 'He takes the credit; I take the blame.'

The role of the **White House chief of staff** is the most critical. Some (e.g. 'Mack' McLarty, 1993–94) have been overwhelmed by the job, possibly because of their own lack of Washington experience. Others (e.g. John Sununu, 1989–92) became far too obtrusive and wanted to become a kind of 'deputy president'. The best model is that of the 'honest broker', 'salesman' and 'javelin catcher' for the president, played well by such people as Leon Panetta (Bill Clinton) and Andrew Card (George W. Bush).

The phrase 'javelin catcher' is attributed to Carter's Chief of Staff, Jack Watson.

3 The National Security Council

Created in 1947, the National Security Council (NSC) was established to help the president coordinate foreign and defence policy. Headed by the National Security Advisor (NSA), the NSC began life as an in-house think-tank for the

Also known as the Pentagon, after the huge five-sided building that houses it.

president. The NSC would gather information, advice and policy options from groups such as:

- the State Department
- the Defense Department
- the Central Intelligence Agency (CIA)
- relevant congressional committees (e.g. Senate Foreign Relations Committee)
- the Joint Chiefs of Staff
- US ambassadors around the world

The NSC would then act as 'honest broker' and 'policy coordinator' to present carefully argued options ready for presidential decision-making.

President Nixon greatly increased the role of the NSA when he appointed Henry Kissinger to the post. Kissinger became a roving foreign policy-maker for the president, largely cutting out the State Department and other agencies, becoming a policy player rather than a mere facilitator. But this new enhanced role for the NSA caused grave problems for both Presidents Carter (over the Iranian hostage crisis) and Reagan (over the Iran–Contra affair). Subsequent NSAs, such as Brent Scowcroft (George H.W. Bush), Sandy Berger (Clinton) and Condoleezza Rice (George W. Bush), have reverted to the more traditional role.

4 The Office of Management and Budget

This was created in 1970 by President Nixon, when he revamped the then Bureau of the Budget.

The two principal functions of the Office of Management and Budget (OMB) are:
(1) to advise the president on the allocation of federal funds in the annual budget
(2) to oversee the spending of all federal government departments and agencies

It is headed by the OMB director, just about the only EXOP post that does require Senate confirmation. Some former OMB directors, such as Leon Panetta for Bill Clinton (1993–94), have provided first-class help and advice for the president on financial and budget matters. Others have proved politically embarrassing (Reagan's David Stockman) or have led the president down disastrous paths (Bush's Richard Darman, who in 1990 advised the president that breaking his 'no new taxes' pledge would not be politically costly in his re-election bid in 2 years' time!).

Darman was known by his critics as 'the prince of darkness'.

E Relations with Congress

Almost every power that the president possesses is checked by Congress. The president, therefore, needs Congress's agreement. But in a system of 'separated institutions, sharing powers' (Neustadt), this is by no means easy. And party links do not help much either. The president and the majority of Congress may be of different parties, as was the case during the last 2 years of

George W. Bush's presidency (2007–08), with a Republican president but the Democrats controlling both houses of Congress.

And even when the two branches are controlled by the same party, this is no guarantee of action — witness the difficulties Bill Clinton experienced in his failed attempt to pass his healthcare reforms in 1993–94. As Richard Neustadt has stated: 'What the Constitution separates, the political parties do not combine.'

But the president needs Congress. As Table 6.8 shows, without it he can do little or nothing. This is all part of the intricate system of 'checks and balances' devised by the Founding Fathers. Professor S.E. Finer has likened the president and Congress to 'two halves of a bank note, each useless without the other.' And the Founding Fathers' desire for cooperation and compromise ('ambition must counteract ambition', as James Madison put it) often leads to inaction and gridlock.

> What the Constitution separates is, of course, the three branches of the federal government.

> What Madison meant by this was that the 'ambition' of the president (i.e. what he wants to do) must be checked by the 'ambition' of Congress (i.e. what it wants to do) and vice versa.

Powers of the president	Checks by Congress
Propose legislation	Amend/block legislation
Submit the annual budget	Amend budget
Veto legislation	Override veto
Nominate executive officials (e.g. cabinet)	**Senate's** power of confirmation
Nominate federal judges	**Senate's** power of confirmation
Negotiate treaties	**Senate's** power of ratification
Commander-in-chief of the armed forces	Declare war/power of the purse
Act as chief executive	Investigation/impeachment/trial/removal

Table 6.8 Powers of the president and checks by Congress

Thus, presidents cannot rely on **formal powers** alone to get what they want. They must also use **informal powers** of persuasion. As Richard Neustadt so succinctly puts it: **'The president's power is the power to persuade.'**

1 *Methods of presidential persuasion*

'I sit here all day trying to persuade people to do the things they ought to have sense enough to do without my persuading them...That's all the powers of the president amount to', famously commented a frustrated President Harry Truman. But Truman was right. So how does a president persuade? There are two methods — through people and through perks.

1.1 Persuasion through people

The president, if he is to be a successful persuader, must work through a number of other people. He cannot — nor should he — try to do it all himself. Who can he use?

> All of the last six VPs (Mondale, Bush, Quayle, Gore, Cheney and Biden) have formerly been members of Congress, which also helps.

- **The vice-president:** as presiding officer of the Senate, he has a foothold in Congress.

- His own **Office of Legislative Affairs:** this is part of the White House Office and those who work here act as full-time lobbyists for the president in Congress.
- **Cabinet officers:** each of these works in their own policy-related areas.
- **Party leaders** in Congress, including the House Speaker, Majority and Minority Leaders in both houses, whips, committee chairs and ranking minority members (see Topic 5.D).

1.2 Persuasion through perks

This works hand-in-hand with the people mentioned above. The president may:
- make **phone calls** to selected members of Congress
- **offer help with legislation** that benefits members' constituents
- **offer help with federal executive/judicial appointments** of interest to constituents
- **invite members to a meeting** at the White House
- **go to Capitol Hill** to address a selected group of members
- **offer to campaign** for members of his own party

And if all else fails, the president can go on national television to **appeal over the heads of members of Congress** directly to the people. This is what President Johnson called 'putting Congress's feet to the fire'.

2 ## The results of presidential persuasion

David Mervin has described the US president as **'bargainer-in-chief'** — and he is. But after all is said and done, the president will be hoping that it will result in his legislation being passed, his appointments confirmed and his treaties ratified. The president's success rate is measured each year in what is called **the presidential support score** (see Table 6.9). This statistic measures how often the president won in roll-call votes in the House and Senate in which he took a clear position, expressed as a percentage of the whole.

President	Year	Support score (%)
Bill Clinton	1993	86.4
	1994	86.4
	1995	36.2
	1996	55.2
	1997	53.6
	1998	50.6
	1999	37.8
	2000	55.0
George W. Bush	2001	87.0
	2002	87.8
	2003	78.7
	2004	72.5
	2005	78.0
	2006	80.9
	2007	38.3
	2008	47.8

Table 6.9 Presidential support score, 1993–2008

Capitol Hill, in Washington DC, is where the building housing Congress stands.

Although the presidential support score is a useful guide to presidential success, keep in mind that:

- the score does not measure the importance of votes
- presidents can avoid low scores by just simply not taking positions on votes they expect to lose
- the score does not count bills which fail even to come to a vote on the floor of either house (e.g. Clinton's healthcare reform bill never came to a vote in either house in 1994 and therefore did not feature in the 86.4% support score recorded that year)

It is also worth keeping in mind that changes in Congress — and more widely in the US political system — make the president's job more difficult these days when trying to build support for his legislation than was the case, say, back in the 1950s and 1960s. There are five reasons for this:

(1) Declining levels of party discipline in Congress.

(2) Less likelihood that the president and a majority of Congress will be of the same party.

(3) House and Senate members being more aware of constituents' wishes (through the effects of C-SPAN and e-mail, for example) and therefore perhaps less willing to go along with what the president wants.

(4) Changes in the methods of selecting presidential candidates, resulting in 'Washington outsiders' becoming president — Governors Carter, Reagan, Clinton and George W. Bush.

(5) The fragmentation of power in Congress, including the declining power of committee chairs and the like.

C-SPAN is the cable television company which gives complete coverage of House and Senate debates.

F Limits on presidential power

Consider the following comments:

- 'Weakness is still what I see; weakness in the sense of a great gap between what is expected of a man (or someday woman) and assured capacity to carry through.' (Richard Neustadt)
- 'The presidency is not a powerful office...Presidents cannot command obedience to their wishes but must persuade.' (James Pfiffner)
- 'It sometimes seems almost miraculous that presidents accomplish anything at all.' (David Mervin)
- 'Leadership is difficult precisely because the framers of the Constitution wanted it to be so...Opportunities to check power abound; opportunities to exercise power are limited.' (Thomas Cronin and Michael Genovese)

Not exactly a vote of confidence for 'the most powerful person in the world' claim! But the more you realise the **limits** on presidential power, the better will be your understanding of the paradoxes of the office of the US presidency.

What are these limits? They can be grouped under eight headings.

1 Congress

Congress can amend/block/delay the president's bills and override his vetoes; the Senate can refuse to confirm his appointments or ratify his treaties; and Congress can investigate, impeach and try him — even remove him from office. (See Topic 5.B.)

2 Supreme Court

It was this case that led to President Clinton having to answer questions posed by Ms Jones's lawyers in January 1998, including ones concerning a possible relationship between the President and a White House employee named Monica Lewinsky. The rest, as they say, is history!

The Supreme Court can declare the president's actions — and those of any member of the executive branch — unconstitutional. Consider the following three examples:
- *United States v. Richard M. Nixon* (1974): the Court declared that President Nixon's refusal to hand over the 'White House tapes' — concerning the Watergate affair — was unconstitutional.
- *William Jefferson Clinton v. Paula Corbin Jones* (1997): the Court declared that President Clinton had to face charges of sexual harassment made by Ms Jones whilst he was still president, rather than waiting until he left office.
- *Rasul v. Bush* (2004): the Supreme Court ruled that the detainees at Guantánamo Bay did have access to the US federal courts to challenge their detention, thereby striking down an important part of the Bush administration's legal policy regarding the war on terror.

3 Public opinion

President Clinton discovered how important public opinion was to being president. He survived his many scandals mainly because his public opinion ratings remained high. President Nixon saw the other side of that coin.

4 Pressure groups

Pressure groups can mobilise public opinion either for or against the president himself or his policies. (See Topic 4.)

5 The media

All modern-day presidents live in an era where the media can profoundly limit what they can do — ask Johnson about Vietnam or Clinton about healthcare reform. The media's coverage of the president as a person is also critical.

6 The federal bureaucracy

The president is only one person in an executive branch made up of 15 executive departments, some 60 other federal government agencies, boards and commissions employing some 3 million civil servants. Getting the federal bureaucracy to do things can be a challenge to any president.

7 Federalism

And it's not just the federal government that limits the president. Many federal government programmes are implemented by state and local governments across the entire USA.

8 Other factors

The president is also often limited by such factors as:
- his own professional reputation
- the quality of his staff
- the unity (or otherwise) of his party and of the opposition
- crises (or the lack of them)
- luck

Questions

1 List the ten powers of the president.

2 What is the 'State of the Union Address'.

3 **(a)** What was George W. Bush's success rate with regular vetoes? **(b)** Was this high or low compared with other presidents?

4 What are the opening (15) words of Article II of the Constitution?

5 Who was the last president to have a treaty rejected by the Senate?

6 **(a)** How many executive departments were there in 1789? **(b)** How many are there now?

7 Give a definition of the president's cabinet.

8 Why do so few cabinet members come from Congress?

9 **(a)** Give four functions that cabinet meetings can perform for the president.
(b) Give four functions that cabinet meetings can perform for cabinet members.

10 Give the six reasons why cabinet meetings can never be all that important.

11 **(a)** Complete the following conclusion of the Brownlow Report in 1939: 'The president…' (2 words); **(b)** What organisation was set up as a result of this report?

12 Give four functions of the White House Office.

13 To what did Professor Finer liken the relationship between the president and Congress?

14 Complete this quotation by Richard Neustadt: 'the president's power is…' (4 words).

15 Who does the president use to persuade members of Congress to support him when they vote?

16 What does the presidential support score measure?

17 Identify the seven main limits on the power of the president.

Article II of the Constitution states that 'in case of the removal of the President from office, or of his death, resignation or inability to discharge the powers and duties of the said office, the same shall devolve on the Vice-President'. That the vice-president may become president gives the office its potential importance. But throughout most of the nineteenth and a good deal of the twentieth century, the office seemed to be a dumping ground for political non-entities — the has-beens, might-have-beens and thought-they-ought-to-have-beens of US politics. The list, after all, does include Hannibal Hamblin (1861–65) and Schuyler Colfax (1869–73). But no longer. Vice-President Dick Cheney (2001–09) was dubbed 'the prime minister' and 'the deputy president'. But Cheney was not the first important vice-president. The office has been growing in importance for decades. In this topic, we shall discover both why and how.

The topic is divided into the following two major headings:

A Selection, election and powers

B The increased importance of the office: why and how

In an article in *The Economist* in March 2001, Vice-President Dick Cheney was described as 'the most powerful vice-president in history'.

A Selection, election and powers

1 Selection of vice-presidential candidates

The selection of the vice-presidential candidate is now done **by the presidential candidate** at — or nowadays usually just before — the party's National Convention (see Topic 2.A.3.2b). Times were when the National Convention itself did the choosing. But this has not occurred in either major party since 1956.

In 1956, Adlai Stevenson allowed the Democratic Convention to choose his running-mate, Senator Estes Kefauver of Tennessee.

In order to be chosen, the vice-presidential candidate must fulfil the same constitutional requirements as for the presidency regarding age, citizenship and residency, and not have already served two terms as president. This is for the simple reason that the vice-president may be called upon to become president.

2 Election of the vice-president

Again, the system has changed. Between 1789 and 1801, the vice-president was elected separately from the president. When the Electoral College votes were counted (see Topic 2.A.5), the winner would become president and the runner-up would become vice-president. This is how the first three vice-presidents — John Adams (1789–97), Thomas Jefferson (1797–1801) and Aaron Burr (1801–05) — were elected. The office was therefore seen as being **'the president in waiting'**. Adams, the first vice-president, became the second president. Jefferson, the second vice-president, became the third president.

The next vice-president to achieve this feat was George H.W. Bush in 1989.

But in 1804, the **12th Amendment** was ratified. From then on, the president and vice-president were elected together — a **'joint ticket'**. The importance of the office declined drastically. Of the next 32 vice-presidents, only one — Martin Van Buren in 1837 — was elected president in his own right, other than those who first came to the office by the death of the president.

3 Appointment of the vice-president

In 1967, another constitutional amendment was passed affecting the office of the vice-presidency. The **25th Amendment**, amongst other things, gave the president the power to fill up vacancies in the vice-presidency. As Table 7.1 shows, for much of the nineteenth and twentieth centuries, the office remained empty. Either the vice-president himself died or the president died and the vice-president became president. Indeed, in the last 50 years of the nineteenth century, there was a vice-president in office for little more than half the time.

Dates	Reason for the vice-presidency being vacant
1812–13	Vice-President George Clinton died in office
1814–17	Vice-President Elbridge Gerry died in office
1832–33	Vice-President John Calhoun resigned to become a US senator
1841–45	President Harrison died; **V-P John Tyler became president**
1850–53	President Taylor died; **V-P Millard Fillmore became president**
1853–57	Vice-President William King died in office
1865–69	President Lincoln assassinated; **V-P Andrew Johnson became president**
1875–77	Vice-President Henry Wilson died in office
1881–85	President Garfield assassinated; **V-P Chester Arthur became president**
1885–89	Vice-President Thomas Hendricks died in office
1899–1901	Vice-President Garret Hobart died in office
1901–05	President McKinley assassinated; **V-P Theodore Roosevelt became president**
1912–13	Vice-President James Sherman died in office
1923–25	President Harding died; **V-P Calvin Coolidge became president**
1945–49	President F.D. Roosevelt died; **V-P Harry Truman became president**
1963–65	President Kennedy assassinated; **V-P Lyndon Johnson became president**

Table 7.1 Vacancies in the vice-presidency, 1812–1965

Do make sure you say 'newly appointed' rather than 'elected'. Congress did not have to confirm Dick Cheney as vice-president in 2001 because he was elected.

This all changed with the 25th Amendment. When, in 1973, Vice-President Spiro Agnew resigned, President Nixon appointed Congressman Gerald Ford of Michigan to fill the post. Within less than a year, Nixon himself resigned over the Watergate affair. Ford became president and he appointed former New York Governor Nelson Rockefeller as the new vice-president. Newly appointed vice-presidents have to be confirmed by a vote in **both** houses of Congress. A simple majority is required in each house. This is the only appointment the House of Representatives gets to confirm.

In his absence, the task is performed by junior senators from the majority party.

On average, a vice-president can expect to cast a vote about once a year.

4 *Constitutional powers*

The vice-president has five constitutional powers:

(1) **Presiding officer of the Senate:** this power involves him in chairing Senate debates, though in practice he will rarely do this.

(2) **Casting a vote in Senate in the case of a tie:** in the 28 years between January 1981 and January 2009, vice-presidents have been called upon to break tied votes on 19 occasions. Al Gore (1993–2001) managed 4 in his 8-year term; Dick Cheney cast 8 tie-breaking votes in his 8 years. In April 2001, Dick Cheney used this power to help pass George W. Bush's $1.6 trillion tax cut.

(3) **Counting the Electoral College votes** and announcing the winner before a joint session of Congress: in January 2001, Vice-President Al Gore had to announce his own defeat in the Electoral College vote at the hands of Governor George W. Bush.

(4) **Becoming president** on the death, resignation or removal from office of the president: this has occurred nine times, eight times by the death of the president (see Table 7.1) and once when Nixon resigned (August 1974).

(5) **Becoming acting president** if the president is declared, or declares himself, disabled: a provision of the 25th Amendment (1967) used only once, when in July 1985, Vice-President George Bush became Acting President for 8 hours whilst President Reagan underwent surgery in a Washington hospital.

With the exception of the fourth power, they do not make an impressive list. The first vice-president, John Adams, famously commented of his office: 'In this I am nothing, but I may be everything.' Others have been even less generous, describing the office as anything from 'not worth a bucket of warm spit' (John Nance Garner, 1933–41) to being 'as useful as a cow's fifth teat' (Harry Truman, 1945).

B The increased importance of the office: why and how

1 *The period of unimportance*

Certainly for much of the nineteenth century and the first half of the twentieth century, the office of vice-president was regarded as unimportant. Amongst the reasons for this were:

- its lack of significant powers
- the passage of the 12th Amendment, depriving the vice-president of election in his own right
- the frequency with which the office remained empty
- between 1804 and the 1950s, it was not seen as an obvious stepping-stone to the presidency, whereas being a senator or a state governor were seen in that way

- presidents were not especially over-burdened with the duties of their office and therefore gave little of significance to their vice-presidents to do

One frustrated occupant of the office commented that he seemed to spend most of his time 'going to funerals', a reference to the fact that vice-presidents were often sent abroad to represent the president at foreign funerals.

2   *The emergence of the 'modern vice-presidency'*

The office of vice-president is clearly now more significant and prestigious than used to be the case. Why and how did this occur?

Some commentators suggest that the turning point was when Harry Truman became president on the death of FDR in 1945. He was shocked by how little he knew of what was going on in the White House. Admittedly, he had been vice-president for little more than 3 months when Roosevelt died, but he did not even know that the USA had developed a nuclear weapon. Truman was determined that never again would a vice-president be kept in such ignorance. The trouble was that for the next 4 years, Truman did not have a vice-president. But it was Truman's vice-president, Alben Barkley (1949–53), who became the first to attend cabinet meetings routinely. Truman also made him a member of the National Security Council.

However, the real change probably came with the Eisenhower–Nixon administration (1953–61). There are a number of reasons for this:
- Nixon was a nationally known figure before becoming vice-president.
- He was only the fifth vice-president to serve 8 years in the office.
- The role of the federal government, and thereby the role of the president, had increased significantly as a result of both Roosevelt's 'New Deal' policies and of the USA's new superpower status.
- President Eisenhower adopted a delegatory approach to the presidency.
- Eisenhower suffered from bouts of ill-health, including a 5-month lay-off recovering from a heart attack.

As a result of this, during his 8 years as vice-president, Nixon:
- chaired 19 cabinet meetings in the president's absence
- visited 54 countries, including high-profile visits to Venezuela (1958) and the USSR (1959)
- came to be regarded as Eisenhower's successor, Eisenhower being the first president to be limited to two terms in office

From this point on, the office gradually emerged as more important and therefore more sought-after:
- **Lyndon Johnson** (1961–63) chaired the president's Commission on Employment Opportunities and took a leading role in progress on civil rights.
- **Hubert Humphrey** (1965–69) was used by Johnson as his major link with local government — Humphrey had been Mayor of Minneapolis — in the enactment of his 'Great Society' programme to improve life in the inner cities.
- **Spiro Agnew** (1969–73) — a former Baltimore City councillor and governor of Maryland — headed Nixon's Office of Intergovernmental Relations.

Later that same year, he used it!

In Venezuela, Nixon's motorcade was attacked by an angry, rock-throwing crowd.

The 22nd Amendment introducing the two-term limit was ratified in 1951, but excluded the then incumbent President Harry Truman.

- **Walter Mondale** (1977–81) became a general policy advisor to President Carter and was the first vice-president to be given a West Wing office and to be shown the Presidential Daily Briefing (PDB) — the intelligence briefing given to the president at the start of each day.

All subsequent vice-presidents have benefited from this piece-by-piece growth in the importance of the office. All vice-presidents now attend cabinet meetings, sit on the NSC, have a West Wing office, see the PDB and so on. No longer is the office a dumping-ground for non entities that it was in decades gone by. The passage of the 25th Amendment, resulting in the fact that the office will now always be occupied, has also had a role in enhancing the status of the office.

Vice-president	Dates	Subsequent political career
Richard Nixon	**1953–61**	Republican presidential candidate 1960; **president 1969–74**
Lyndon Johnson	**1961–63**	**President 1963–69**
Hubert Humphrey	1965–69	Democratic presidential candidate 1968
Spiro Agnew	1969–73	–
Gerald Ford	**1973–74**	**President 1974–77**
Nelson Rockefeller	1974–77	(Had contested Republican presidential primaries in 1968)
Walter Mondale	1977–81	Democratic presidential candidate 1984
George H.W. Bush	**1981–89**	**President 1989–93**
Dan Quayle	1989–93	–
Al Gore	1993–2001	Democratic presidential candidate 2000
Dick Cheney	2001–09	–

Table 7.2 Subsequent political careers of vice-presidents, from Nixon to Cheney

As Table 7.2 shows, the last 11 vice-presidents (not counting Joe Biden) have included four presidents-to-be — Nixon, Johnson, Ford and George H.W. Bush. Of the remaining six, three became the presidential candidates of their party — Humphrey, Mondale and Gore. Another — Nelson Rockefeller — had previously run in the presidential primaries.

Add to this fact that, of the last six presidents, four — Carter, Reagan, Clinton and George W. Bush — have been Washington 'outsiders'. They had never before held political office in Washington, serving only as state governors. Their respective vice-presidents — Mondale, George H.W. Bush, Gore and Cheney — were all Washington 'insiders'. It is this that gave Dick Cheney his importance in the Bush administration. Cheney — a former White House Chief of Staff, Congressman and Secretary of Defense — was seen as the person to help President George W. Bush get things done in Washington.

'It is no exaggeration to say that there is a new vice-presidency. [It is] a highly visible office that is increasingly recognised as a springboard to the presidency.' (Paul Light, *Vice Presidential Power*, 1984)

Questions

1 (a) Who selects the vice-presidential candidate? **(b)** When does this usually occur?

2 How is the vice-president elected nowadays?

3 Which two vice-presidents were appointed to office following the passage of the 25th Amendment?

4 What are the five constitutional powers of the vice-president?

5 Complete this quotation by Vice-President John Adams: 'In this I am nothing, but…' (4 words).

6 Who was the first twentieth-century vice-president to be regarded as significant?

7 Which vice-presidents since 1952 have gone on to become president?

8 Which other vice-presidents since 1952 have gone on to become their party's presidential candidate — though they lost the election?

The third branch of the federal government is the judiciary, which enforces and interprets the law. There are three tiers of courts: the trial courts, the appeal courts and the Supreme Court. We need concern ourselves with only the Supreme Court.

The Supreme Court is important for two reasons. First, its **members hold office for life** and, second, its functions include not only interpreting federal laws, but also **interpreting the Constitution**. By its power of **judicial review**, the Supreme Court can strike down laws passed by Congress — as well as state laws — by declaring them unconstitutional. This is a highly significant power, with political implications. However, just as with the other two branches of government, the Supreme Court does have a number of checks upon it.

The topic is divided into the following four major headings:

A The justices

B The power of judicial review

C The Supreme Court and the protection of rights and liberties

D Checks on the Supreme Court

A The justices

1 Membership

There are a number of key points to remember regarding the membership of and the appointment process to the Supreme Court:

- There are **nine members** of the Supreme Court: one chief justice; eight associate justices (see Table 8.1).
- The number is fixed by Congress and has remained unchanged since 1869.
- They are **appointed by the president**.
- They must be **confirmed by the Senate**.
- They **hold office for life** 'during good behaviour' (Article III, Section 1), meaning they can be impeached, tried and removed from office by Congress; otherwise justices leave the Court only by voluntary retirement or death.

Franklin Roosevelt tried to increase the number, but Congress refused to agree to it.

2 Appointment process

The appointment process is conducted as follows:

(1) The president must wait for a vacancy to occur: on average about once every 2 years, though Carter (1977–81) made no appointments and no vacancies occurred between 1994 and 2005.

(2) The president's closest aides begin the search for suitable candidates.

(3) A short list is drawn up and candidates are subjected to a detailed interview and FBI background checks.

Justice	Date appointed	President appointing
Chief Justice:		
John Roberts	2005	George W. Bush (R)
Associate Justices:		
John Paul Stevens	1975	Gerald Ford (R)
Antonin Scalia	1986	Ronald Reagan (R)
Anthony Kennedy	1988	Ronald Reagan (R)
Clarence Thomas	1991	George H.W. Bush (R)
Ruth Bader Ginsburg	1993	Bill Clinton (D)
Stephen Breyer	1994	Bill Clinton (D)
Samuel Alito	2006	George W. Bush (R)
Sonia Sotomayor	2009	Barack Obama

Table 8.1 Supreme Court membership (2009)

(4) The president announces the nominee at a public gathering at the White House.

(5) The American Bar Association (ABA) traditionally offered a professional rating of the nominee (see Table 8.2):
- 'well qualified'
- 'qualified'
- 'not qualified'

(6) The nominee (plus other witnesses) appears before a hearing at the Senate Judiciary Committee.

(7) The Senate Judiciary Committee votes on whether or not to recommend confirmation.

(8) The nomination is debated on the floor of the Senate.

(9) A final vote is taken — a **simple majority** is required for confirmation.

The Senate Judiciary Committee's vote is only a recommendation, though it is rarely overturned.

Nominee	Year	ABA rating	Senate Judiciary Committee vote	Senate vote
Robert Bork	1987	Well qualified	5–9	42–58
David Souter	1990	Well qualified	13–1	90–9
Clarence Thomas	1991	Qualified	7–7	52–48
Ruth Bader Ginsburg	1993	Well qualified	18–0	96–3

Table 8.2 ABA ratings and Senate votes on selected Supreme Court nominees

When the president is searching for a new member of the Supreme Court, where will he look? There are five possible pools of recruitment:
- The federal Appeals Court (e.g. Clarence Thomas, 1991)
- The state courts (e.g. Sandra Day O'Connor, 1981–2006)

- The executive branch (e.g. William Rehnquist, 1971–2005)
- Academia (e.g. a law professor at a prestigious university)
- Congress (e.g. a member of the Senate Judiciary Committee)

The Senate has rejected 12 Supreme Court nominees since 1789, the most recent being that of Robert Bork in 1987. Before that, President Nixon lost two nominees in as many years — Clement Haynsworth (45–55) in 1969 and Harrold Carswell (45–51) in 1970. In 1987, Douglas Ginsburg withdrew from the nomination after admitting illegal drug use during his confirmation hearing at the Senate Judiciary Committee.

3 Philosophy of justices

It is often suggested that presidents look for justices who share their judicial philosophy. In this respect, justices are classified as to whether they are 'liberals' or 'conservatives'. Another classification used is of **'loose constructionists'** and **'strict constructionists'** (see Table 8.3).

These are technical, legal terms. Think of the word 'construction' as meaning 'interpretation'.

Classification	Ideology	Characteristics	Party	Examples
Strict constructionists	Conservative	Strict/literal interpretation of the Constitution; favour states' rights	Tend to be appointed by Republican presidents	Roberts Scalia Thomas Alito
Loose constructionists	Liberal	Read things into the Constitution; favour federal government power	Tend to be appointed by Democratic presidents	Ginsburg Breyer Sotomayor

Table 8.3 Classification of Supreme Court justices

There are exceptions. President George H.W. Bush did not realise when he appointed David Souter to the Court in 1990 that he was appointing one of its most liberal members. Other justices — like Anthony Kennedy — are much less easy to classify. They tend to be referred to as **'swing' justices**.

B The power of judicial review

1 Definition and origins

Don't bother to get into the details of this case — they are not important.

Judicial review is the power of the Supreme Court to declare acts of Congress, or actions of the executive — or acts or actions of state governments — unconstitutional, and thereby null and void. This power is nowhere mentioned in the Constitution. One might say that the Court 'found' the power for itself in the 1803 case of *Marbury v. Madison*. This was the first time that the Supreme Court declared an act of Congress unconstitutional.

2 *Usage*

'Strict constructionists' tend to favour 'judicial restraint'; 'loose constructionists' tend to favour 'judicial activism' — but note the word 'tend'.

Since then, the Supreme Court has used this power on hundreds of occasions — at times sparingly (periods of **'judicial restraint'**), but at other times far more frequently (periods of **'judicial activism'**). By using its power of judicial review, the Court can, in effect, update the meaning of the words of the Constitution, most of which were written over two centuries ago. Hence, they will decide what the phrase in the 8th Amendment (written in 1791) forbidding 'cruel and unusual punishments' means today. Likewise, they will decide whether the 1st Amendment right of 'freedom of speech' applies to the Internet. As a former Chief Justice, Charles Evans Hughes, once remarked: 'We are under a Constitution, but the Constitution is what the judges say it is.'

3 *Political importance*

Using its power of judicial review, the Supreme Court has involved itself in a host of political issues. It is this that helps give the Court its political importance because many of the issues dealt with by the Court are the hot-button political issues of the day, matters over which political parties disagree and elections are fought.

A common focus for essay questions. Don't forget to deal with the appointment process and the power of judicial review — both are important here.

The Supreme Court can also be seen as something of a 'political body' because its members are appointed by a politician (the president) and confirmed by other politicians (senators). Appointments to the Supreme Court also become an issue in many presidential elections. This was certainly the case in the 2000 election.

One can see very clearly — some might say too clearly — the political importance of the Supreme Court in the case of *George W. Bush v. Albert Gore Jr* (2000). Five weeks after the presidential election, on 11 December 2000, the Supreme Court ruled that the manual recount scheme devised by the Florida Supreme Court was unconstitutional because it violated the 'equal protection' clause of the 14th Amendment. In the same decision, the Court also ruled that given the time constraints, 'it is evident that any recount seeking to meet the December 12 [deadline] will be unconstitutional'. The Court was seen by some to be literally handing the election to Governor Bush.

In recent decades, the Supreme Court has, for example, handed down judgements of great political significance in such areas as:
- the rights of racial minorities
- the rights of arrested persons
- capital punishment
- abortion rights
- freedom of religion
- freedom of speech, freedom of the press and freedom of expression
- gun control
- the actions of the executive branch, including the president

c The Supreme Court and the protection of rights and liberties

1 ### Freedom of religion

The term 'public school' in the USA is equivalent to 'state school' in the UK.

'Graduation ceremonies' in US schools are ceremonies for students at the end of their school career.

- *Engel v. Vitale* (1962): the Court, in nullifying a New York state law, declared that government-sponsored prayer in public schools violated the 1st Amendment clause against 'an establishment of religion'.
- *Wallace v. Jaffree* (1985): the Court declared an Alabama state law providing for a period of silent meditation at the start of the school day in public schools to be unconstitutional.
- *Lee v. Weisman* (1992): the Court declared prayer at public school graduation ceremonies unconstitutional.
- *Allegheny County v. American Civil Liberties Union* (1989): the Court declared Allegheny (Pennsylvania) County's Christmas display an infringement of 1st Amendment rights because it contained only religious figures, whereas in 1984 (*Lynch v. Donnelly*) the Court had okayed the City of Pawtucket's (Rhode Island) display, which included religious figures but also Santa Claus and a Christmas tree.
- *Zelman v. Simmons–Harris* (2002): the Court upheld Ohio's so-called 'school voucher' programme.
- *McCreary County, Kentucky v. ACLU* (2005) and *Van Orden v. Perry* (2005): the Court ruled on the display of the ten commandments in public places, finding the Kentucky commandments unconstitutional but the Texas ones (*Van Orden*) constitutional.

2 ### Freedom of speech and expression

President George H.W. Bush described the Court's decision as 'wrong, dead wrong'.

The *Washington Post* headlined the decision as 'The First Amendment Goes Digital'.

- *Rankin v. McPherson* (1987): the Court upheld the right of Ardith McPherson not to be sacked for making comments about the assassination attempt on President Reagan in 1981, claiming that her 1st Amendment rights of freedom of speech had been infringed.
- *Texas v. Johnson* (1989): a Texas state law forbidding the burning of the US flag was declared unconstitutional by the Court.
- *United States v. Eichman* (1990): the 1989 Flag Protection Act was declared unconstitutional.
- *Reno v. American Civil Liberties Union* (1997): the 1996 Communications Decency Act was declared unconstitutional. The Act made it a crime to make 'indecent' or 'patently offensive' material available to minors on the Internet. But the Court claimed that this infringed the 1st Amendment rights of adults because the law was too vague in its definitions.

- *Ashcroft v. Free Speech Coalition* **(2002):** the Court declared the Child Pornography Protection Act of 1996 unconstitutional.
- *Watchtower Bible and Tract Society v. Village of Stratton,* Ohio **(2002):** the Court struck down a law which required people going door-to-door — whether salespersons, politicians or representatives of religious groups — to get a permit beforehand.

3 The right to bear arms

- *United States v. Lopez* **(1995):** the Court declared unconstitutional the 1990 Gun-Free School Zones Act, stating that Congress had exceeded its power under Article I, Section 8. This case was one that also had clear implications for the scope of federal government power over state and local jurisdictions.
- *Printz v. United States* **(1997):** the Court declared unconstitutional part of the 1993 Brady Act requiring local law enforcement officers to conduct background checks on would-be hand-gun purchasers during a 5-day waiting period. Here was another ruling clearly affecting the federal–state government balance.
- *District of Columbia v. Heller* **(2008):** the Court declared unconstitutional a law passed by the District of Columbia in 1976 banning the ownership of handguns and requiring shotguns and rifles be kept unloaded and either disassembled or trigger-locked. The Court stated for the first time that, in its interpretation, the 2nd Amendment right to 'keep and bear arms' is an individual, rather than merely a collective, right.

4 The rights of arrested persons

- *Gideon v. Wainwright* **(1963):** the Court interpreted the 14th Amendment as guaranteeing the right to legal representation.
- *Miranda v. Arizona* **(1966):** the Court interpreted the 5th Amendment right to remain silent as extending to the right to be reminded of that right when arrested.

5 Capital punishment

- *Furman v. Georgia* **(1972):** the Court decided that the death penalty, as then imposed, was a 'cruel and unusual punishment' and thereby violated the 8th Amendment. The consequences of this case included the more widespread use of lethal injection and of two-stage trials, in which, during a second stage, mitigating circumstances are considered before the sentence is decided.
- *Atkins v. Virginia* **(2002):** the Court ruled that the execution of mentally retarded criminals was unconstitutional.
- *Roper v. Simmons* **(2005):** the Court ruled that it was unconstitutional to sentence anyone to death for a crime they committed when younger than 18.
- *Baze v. Rees* **(2008):** the Court decided that lethal injection — the method used by the federal government and 35 states to execute criminals — did not violate the 8th Amendment ban on 'cruel and unusual punishment'.

'Miranda rights', as the police now call them, have probably featured in a number of US-made crime films you might have seen.

It is important to include the phrase 'as then imposed'. The case did not declare capital punishment *per se* to be unconstitutional.

6

The rights of racial minorities

When using these cases in an answer, don't get side-tracked by the narrative. What happened to whom is really not important. Concentrate on the analytical importance of the case.

This case led to the 1957 showdown in Little Rock, Arkansas, resulting in federal troops being sent by President Eisenhower to enforce the Court's decision.

- **Brown v. The Board of Education of Topeka (1954):** the Court declared a law of the state of Kansas to be unconstitutional because it transgressed the 'equal protection' clause of the 14th Amendment. It led to the desegregation of schools across the USA, especially in the Deep South. 'Separate educational facilities are inherently unequal', declared the Court, overturning its 1896 ruling of 'separate but equal'.

- **Swann v. Charlotte–Mecklenberg Board of Education (1971):** the Court extended the ban on segregated schools from *de jure* segregation (mainly in the South) to *de facto* segregation (mainly in the cities of the Northeast) caused by the widespread policy of neighbourhood schooling. It led to the introduction of school busing programmes to provide racially mixed schools in all areas.

This case led to wide-spread anti-busing protests in many US cities in the Northeast, notably Boston, where protesters burnt the buses — thankfully before the children were on board!

- **Adarand Constructors v. Peña (1995):** the Court struck down a federal government affirmative action programme on the employment of minority workers. This case led to President Clinton's remark about affirmative action: 'Mend it, don't end it.'

- **Gratz v. Bollinger (2003):** the Court ruled that the University of Michigan's affirmative action-based undergraduate admissions programme was unconstitutional because it was too 'mechanistic'.

- **Parents Involved in Community Schools Inc. v. Seattle School District (2007)** and **Meredith v. Jefferson County (Kentucky) Board of Education (2007):** the Court declared it unconstitutional to assign students to public schools solely for the purpose of achieving racial balance.

7

Abortion rights

The phrase 'personal choice' gives rise to those who support abortion rights calling themselves 'pro-choice'.

- **Roe v. Wade (1973):** the Court struck down a Texas state law forbidding abortion. It interpreted the 14th Amendment right of 'liberty' to include 'freedom of personal choice in matters of marriage and family life', and that this right 'necessarily includes the right of a woman to decide whether or not to terminate her pregnancy'. Few cases have been of such profound political importance.

- **Webster v. Reproductive Health Services (1989):** the Court upheld a state law of Missouri forbidding the involvement of any 'public employee' or 'public facility' in the performance of an abortion 'not necessary to save the life of the mother'. Pro-choice supporters regarded this as the Court nibbling away at *Roe v. Wade*.

- **Planned Parenthood of Southeastern Pennsylvania v. Casey (1992):** the Court upheld a Pennsylvania state law that required a married woman seeking an abortion to receive counselling on the risks and alternatives and to wait 24 hours after receiving counselling. Women under 18 also had to

'Pro-life' = anti-abortionists.

have parental consent for an abortion. This again was opposed by the pro-choice lobby. But the pro-life supporters were also angry, as they wanted the Court to go all the way and overturn *Roe v. Wade*. However, the Court struck down the provision in the Pennsylvania state law which required a married woman to notify her spouse before undergoing an abortion.

- *Gonzales v. Carhart* **(2007):** the Court upheld the Partial-Birth Abortion Ban Act passed by Congress in 2003. This was the first time the Court had declared that a specific abortion procedure could be banned and made no exception for the health of the woman, although it did provide an exception if the life of the mother was threatened.

D Checks on the Supreme Court

1 *By Congress*

- The Senate confirms all Supreme Court appointments.
- The House can impeach justices and the Senate try them and, if found guilty by a two-thirds majority, remove them from office.
- Congress can alter the number of justices on the Court.
- Congress can initiate constitutional amendments, thereby seeking to overturn judgements of the Court with which it disagrees, such as recent (though unsuccessful) attempts concerning flag desecration, school prayers, abortion rights and congressional term limits.

2 *By the president*

- Nominates all justices.
- Can decide either to throw his political weight behind the Court (e.g. Eisenhower over the 1954 *Brown v. Board* decision) or to criticise it openly (e.g. Nixon over 'busing' in 1972 and George H.W. Bush over flag-burning in 1990).
- Has the power of pardon (see Topic 6.A.10).

3 *Other checks*

- The Court has no enforcement powers (e.g. in the *Brown v. Board* decision it was dependent upon Eisenhower sending in federal troops to desegregate the Little Rock Central High School in 1957).
- The Court has no initiation power. It has to wait for cases to come before it. It cannot rule on hypothetical issues.
- Public opinion can sometimes be seen as a check on the Court (e.g. the *Casey* decision on abortion rights in 1992).
- The Constitution itself — some parts of the document are unambiguous and not open to interpretation.

- The Supreme Court may check itself by reversing earlier decisions. Having ruled in 1989 (*Stanford v. Kentucky*) that states could execute 16- and 17-year-old offenders, the Court ruled in 2003 (*Roper v. Simmons*) that such executions were unconstitutional. In 2000 (*Stenberg v. Carhart*), the Court declared a Nebraska state law prohibiting late-term abortions to be unconstitutional, but in 2007 (*Gonzales v. Carhart*) upheld an almost identical federal law.

Questions

1 How many members are there on the Supreme Court?

2 **(a)** Who appoints them? **(b)** Who must confirm them? **(c)** For how long do they hold office?

3 Which committee begins the confirmation of judges?

4 **(a)** Who is currently the Chief Justice of the United States? **(b)** By whom was he appointed?

5 Explain the terms: **(a)** strict constructionists; **(b)** loose constructionists.

6 Who is seen on the current Supreme Court as the 'swing justice'?

7 Define judicial review.

8 Complete the following quotation by Charles Evans Hughes: 'We are under a Constitution, but the Constitution is…' (6 words).

9 What was significant about the decision in *District of Columbia v. Heller* (2008)?

10 What was significant about the decision in *Gonzales v. Carhart* (2007)?

11 What checks exist on the power of the Supreme Court?

TOPIC 9 Racial and ethnic politics

The USA is a nation of great ethnic diversity. We have seen the importance and consequences of this in a number of the topics we have studied: the way ethnic minorities vote in elections; the support they give to political parties; pressure groups that work for the interests of ethnic and racial groups; representation in Congress of racial minorities; the racial make-up of the federal government; appointments to the Supreme Court; the protection of rights and liberties of African-Americans. Given the ethnic diversity of American society and the waves of immigrants that have arrived in the country over the centuries, one can hardly gain a full appreciation of the way the US is governed without a study of racial and ethnic politics.

This topic is divided into the following four major headings:

A The civil rights movement

B Affirmative action

C Minority representation in government

D Protection of rights and liberties of racial and ethnic minorities

A The civil rights movement

Specifically the 13th, 14th and 15th Amendments.

The phrase comes from an 1896 Supreme Court ruling.

The civil rights movement grew out of the 1950s. The post-civil war period had seen the passage of constitutional amendments guaranteeing rights for African-Americans, but laws in many states — especially in the Deep South — meant that these rights were not a reality for most blacks. Whether in schools, housing, job recruitment, public transport or leisure facilities, blacks were still **'separate but equal'** at best, a discriminated against and persecuted minority at worst.

The civil rights movement was initially characterised by peaceful protest against government-sponsored segregation and was played out on the streets and in the court rooms, rather than in the debating chambers of Congress or the federal offices of Washington DC.

See Topic 8.C.6.

The highlights of the movement included:
- the Supreme Court's ruling in *Brown v. Board of Education of Topeka* (1954)
- the bus boycotts and freedom riders in the South following the arrest of Rosa Parks (1955)
- the March for Jobs and Freedom in Washington DC, including Martin Luther King's 'I have a dream' speech (1963)
- the assassination of Martin Luther King (1968)
- government-sponsored programmes to assist ethnic minorities including busing, quotas and affirmative action
- the Million Man March in Washington DC (1995)

The civil rights movement was divided into a number of differing factions, some peaceful, some violent, each with their own leaders, including:
- Martin Luther King and the Southern Christian Leadership Conference
- Malcolm X and (later) Louis Farrakhan and the Nation of Islam movement

- Jesse Jackson and the National Rainbow Coalition
- the National Association for the Advancement of Colored People (NAACP)

B Affirmative action

1 Brief history

The debate centres around whether society should be aiming for **'equality of opportunity'** or **'equality of results'**. From the mid-twentieth century, many civil rights advocates came to believe that 'equality of opportunity' would not in itself guarantee equality for minority groups. They would only have rights in theory, not in practice. Only 'equality of results' would truly deliver equality for racial and ethnic minorities. Hence the movement towards what would become known as **affirmative action programmes**.

Affirmative action is a programme that entails giving the members of a previously disadvantaged minority group a head start in such areas as higher education and employment. The term is often regarded as being synonymous with 'positive discrimination'.

In March 1961, President Kennedy created the Equal Employment Opportunity Council (EEOC). Kennedy ordered that projects financed with federal funds 'take affirmative action' to ensure that hiring and employment practices would be free from racial bias. President Johnson used the same phrase in 1965 regarding federal government contractors.

But affirmative action soon attracted its critics. Many regarded 'set asides' and 'quotas' as unfair to those of the majority group — whites — and patronising to those of the minority. Some used the term **'reverse discrimination'** — a term closely associated with the 1978 Supreme Court of *Regents of the University of California v. Bakke* which concerned a white medical student, Allan Bakke, who had been denied a place at the University of California's Medical School, despite the fact that lesser qualified minority students were admitted. Other landmark Supreme Court cases on affirmative action included:

- *Adarand Constructors v. Peña* (1995)
- *Gratz v. Bollinger* (2003)
- *Grutter v. Bollinger* (2003)
- *Parents Involved in Community Schools Inc. v. Seattle School District* (2007)
- *Meredith v. Jefferson County (Kentucky) Board of Education* (2007)

James Q. Wilson and John DiLulio (*American Government*, 2001) summarise the position on affirmative action as follows:

- The Courts will subject any quota system created by state or local governments to 'strict scrutiny' and will be looking for a 'compelling' justification for it.
- Quotas or preference systems cannot be used by state or local governments without first showing that such rules are needed to correct an actual past or present pattern of discrimination.
- In proving that there has been discrimination, it is not enough to show that racial or ethnic minorities are statistically underrepresented among employees etc.

Landmark Supreme Court cases are also discussed in Topic 8.C.6.

- Quotas or preference systems that are created by federal, rather than state, law will be given greater deference.

2 *Arguments for and against affirmative action*

Good essay planning material here!

There are six arguments put forward in favour of affirmative action. They are that affirmative action:
(1) Leads to greater levels of diversity which would not otherwise be achieved.
(2) Rights previous wrongs — the previously disadvantaged are now advantaged.
(3) Opens up areas of education and employment which minorities would not otherwise have considered.
(4) Creates a diverse student body in educational establishments which promotes racial tolerance.
(5) Is the most effective way of delivering equality of opportunity.
(6) Works — for example, between 1960 and 1995, the percentage of blacks aged 25–29 who graduated from university rose from 5% to 15%.

There are six arguments put forward against affirmative action. They are that:
(1) Advantage or preference for one group leads inevitably to disadvantage for another group — the issue of 'reverse discrimination'.
(2) Affirmative action can lead minorities to be admitted to courses or given jobs for which they are ill-equipped to cope.
(3) Such programmes can be condescending to minorities, implying that they need extra help to succeed, thereby demeaning their achievements.
(4) Affirmative action perpetuates a society based on colour and race, thereby encouraging prejudice.
(5) It is no more than a quota system under another name.
(6) It focuses on groups rather than individuals.

3 *Has affirmative action been a success?*

In 1995, President Clinton declared that 'affirmative action has been good for America'. Was he right in this? Has affirmative action been a success in the USA? Before answering that, we must first establish what it was meant to achieve. Affirmative action was meant to move society towards a time when previously disadvantaged groups would no longer be disadvantaged and therefore such programmes would no longer be required. Affirmative action programmes are therefore best seen as a means to an end, not as an end in themselves. So how successful have such programmes been by this measure? There is evidence on both sides.

Some argue that affirmative action programmes have failed and are bound to fail, because a programme that is based on race is unlikely to move society to a point where race no longer counts. But others argue that by promoting diversity, racial tolerance has been enhanced and that old prejudices are slowly dying. The election of Barack Obama as president of the USA would doubtless be presented as evidence that society is moving on from its once ingrained prejudices.

One must also bear in mind whether the costs of affirmative action programmes outweigh their benefits. If, after all, under-prepared blacks or Hispanics are put into academic institutions or jobs where they do not succeed, then the cost may be too high and the programme seen as a failure. If many Americans refuse to visit a black doctor or dentist because they assume that he or she was admitted to medical school and to the position they now hold through quotas rather than qualifications, then the cost may be too high. Some research has found evidence of such problems.

Furthermore, affirmative action can be something of a blunt instrument, one that is too undiscriminating. After all, why should the daughters of the 44th president of the USA be admitted to college ahead of the son or daughter of a West Virginian coal miner?

In the 2003 *Bollinger* decisions, the Supreme Court suggested that affirmative action programmes ought to have a shelf life of a further 25 years. By that reckoning, we shall be better able to judge the success or failure of affirmative action programmes in 2028!

C Minority representation in government

In 1992, President-elect Bill Clinton talked about having a cabinet that 'looks like America'. To what extent do the various branches of the federal government — and, indeed, government at the state and local level — 'look like America' in terms of minority representation?

1 Minorities in Congress

In 1984, there were 21 African-Americans in Congress — all in the House of Representatives. In 2008, as Senator Barack Obama ran for the presidency, there were 41 African-American members of Congress — 40 in the House, and Obama in the Senate. African-American James Clyburn of South Carolina was Majority Whip in the House of Representatives, and five House committee chairmanships were filled by African-Americans. The rise in African-American members of the House was brought about largely by the creation in some states of majority–minority districts in the early 1990s. In 2008, there were also 26 Hispanics in Congress — 23 in the House and three in the Senate, and five Asian-Americans — three in the House, two in the Senate.

2 Minorities and presidential elections

The last 40 years have witnessed the following milestones in African-Americans running for the presidency:
- **1972:** Representative Shirley Chisholm (D) became the first major party African-American candidate for the presidency. She won 152 delegates at her party's National Convention.

- **1984:** Civil rights activist Jesse Jackson (D) won over 3 million votes in the Democratic primaries, finishing third in the number of votes cast. Jackson became the first African-American candidate to win a major party presidential primary, winning contests in four states plus the District of Columbia.
- **1988:** Jackson ran again for the Democratic presidential nomination, this time winning contests in ten states plus Washington DC.
- **2008:** Senator Barack Obama (D) became the first black major party presidential candidate and went on to defeat Republican John McCain to win the presidency.

Between 1992 and 2008, African-American voters gave at least 83% of their votes to the Democratic presidential candidate, rising to 95% in 2008. During the same period, Hispanic voters gave at least 62% of their votes to the Democratic presidential candidate in four of the five elections held in those 16 years. The only election in which the Hispanic vote for the Democrats fell below that figure was 2004, when John Kerry attracted only 57% of the Hispanic vote, with Spanish-speaking Republican President George W. Bush capturing 43% of the Hispanic vote. But that figure fell back dramatically to just 31% for Republican John McCain in 2008 with the Democrat vote up to 67%.

3 Minorities in the executive branch

Minority representation in the president's cabinet first became an issue in modern times when President Lyndon Johnson appointed African-American Robert Weaver as Secretary of Housing and Urban Development in 1966. Between 1966 and 2009, 16 other African-Americans have been appointed to head executive departments, including two of the last three secretaries of state — Colin Powell (2001–05) and Condoleezza Rice (2005–09) — and Barack Obama's Attorney General, Eric Holder.

Obama's incoming cabinet in January 2009 was the most racially diverse of any administration, with heads of seven of the 15 executive departments being from racial minorities:
- **African-American:** Eric Holder (Justice)
- **Hispanics:** Ken Salazar (Interior) and Hilda Solis (Labor)
- **Chinese-Americans:** Steven Chu (Energy) and Gary Locke (Commerce)
- **Japanese-American:** Eric Shinseki (Veterans Affairs)
- **Lebanese-American:** Ray LaHood (Transportation)

Meanwhile, the federal civil service as a whole has become less white. In 1990, 72.7% of the federal civil service were white; by 2006 this had fallen to 67.9%.

4 Minorities and the judiciary

Not only did President Lyndon Johnson appoint the first African-American to the cabinet, but in 1967 he also appointed the first African-American to the Supreme Court — Thurgood Marshall. Upon Marshall's retirement in 1991, President George H.W. Bush replaced him with another African-American, Clarence Thomas. In 1986, President Ronald Reagan had appointed the first

The media concentrate only on Supreme Court appointments, but appointments to the lower courts of the federal government are important too. They are, after all, the main recruitment pool for justices to the Supreme Court and most cases which come to the Supreme Court have been heard first by the lower federal courts.

Italian-American to the Supreme Court — Antonin Scalia. In 2006, he was joined by fellow Italian-American Samuel Alito, and in 2009 by the first Hispanic on the Supreme Court, Sonia Sotomayor.

But the president who did the most to appoint minority judges to the federal judiciary was Jimmy Carter (1977–81). Carter never made any appointments to the US Supreme Court. No vacancies occurred during his 4-year term. But over 20% of his appointments to the trial and appeal courts of the federal judiciary were from racial minorities. President George W. Bush significantly improved the representation of Hispanics in the federal judiciary. Almost 10% of his appointees were Hispanics.

5 Minorities in state and local government

In 1990, Douglas Wilder (D) became the first African-American to be elected as a state governor when he was elected Governor of Virginia. Since then, both Massachusetts and New York have had black governors — though only Deval Patrick of Massachusetts was elected to the post, New York's David Paterson succeeding to the governorship on the resignation of his predecessor Elliot Spitzer.

In 2008, African-Americans made up 8% of state legislators but with considerable variations amongst the states. There are 11 states, including Idaho and Maine, with no African-American members at all in the state legislature. But then the proportion of African-Americans statewide is less than 1% in both states. At the other end of the scale is Mississippi, where African-Americans make up 36% of the population and 25% of the state legislature.

In 1967, Carl Stokes became the first black mayor of a major US city when he was elected Mayor of Cleveland, Ohio. By 2000, there were 480 black mayors in the USA.

This has been discussed in Topic 8.C.6.

D Protection of rights and liberties of racial and ethnic minorities

Racial and ethnic minorities can look to all three branches of the federal government — as well as to state governments — to protect their rights and liberties. But it is the United States **Supreme Court** which plays the most important role in this matter.

Congress also has a role to play. In 1957, Congress passed a law to create the Civil Rights Commission, making it a federal crime to prevent a person from voting in a federal election. Congress passed further important civil rights legislation in 1964 and 1965, improving the civil rights of African-Americans in such areas as voting, education and employment. They followed this with the passage of the 1968 Civil Rights Act which dealt principally with discrimination in housing.

The **president** has also had a role to play in this area. President Eisenhower sent federal troops to Little Rock, Arkansas, in 1957 to enforce the desegregation of the city's Central High School. Both Presidents Kennedy (1961–63) and Johnson (1963–69) used their position to push for civil rights reform during the 1960s. President Clinton (1993–2001) conducted a public debate about the role of affirmative action in the USA. And President George W. Bush (2001–09) publicly supported the Supreme Court's decision in *Gratz v. Bollinger* in 2003. The three most recent presidents — Bill Clinton, George W. Bush and Barack Obama — have all advanced the cause of racial minorities through their federal government appointments, most notably to their cabinets.

Questions

1 Define affirmative action.

2 What is 'reverse discrimination'?

3 Name three recent Supreme Court decisions which have dealt with affirmative action.

4 What six arguments are put forward in favour of affirmative action?

5 What six arguments are put forward against affirmative action?

6 Complete the following quotation by President Clinton in 1995: 'Affirmative action has been…' (3 words).

7 How many **(a)** African-Americans and **(b)** Hispanics were elected to Congress in 2008?

8 Who was the African-American civil rights activist who ran for the presidential nomination of the Democratic Party in both 1984 and 1988?

9 Name two of Obama's original (2009) cabinet members who came from racial minorities.

10 **(a)** Who was the first African-American member of the Supreme Court? **(b)** When and by whom was he appointed?

Key political concepts

Your study of American government and politics has followed on from — or may have been in parallel with — a study of the government and politics of the United Kingdom. The danger is that you may not have made as many connections between the two as you could. At various appropriate places in these Revision Notes, comparisons have been drawn upon from the UK. You should seek to do so in your essays.

The A2 examinations include an element of **synoptic assessment**. Synoptic assessment involves the explicit drawing together of knowledge, understanding and skills learned in different parts of your AS and A2 courses in government and politics.

One thing that will help you in this 'drawing together' will be to keep in mind some **key political concepts** that are central to both US government and politics and to the government and politics of the UK and other western European democracies.

This topic deals with seven key political concepts:

A Accountability

B Authority

C Power

D Democracy

E Representation

F Rights

G Pluralism

A Accountability

Juvenal's famous question *'quis custodiet ipsos custodes?'* — 'who will guard the guardians?' — is about accountability.

Politicians are meant to be 'accountable'. Accountability is best thought of as **being answerable** or, if you prefer, **answerability**. It implies that those in positions of power have a duty to explain their actions and open themselves to potential criticism. But the word 'accountability' raises a number of subsidiary questions. To whom are they accountable? How are they accountable? For what are they accountable? Essentially, they are responsible to 'the people', or more specifically 'the electorate'. This gives a clue to the answer to the second question, for one of the means of accountability is through elections. But it is more than that. In a democratic system of government characterised by the doctrine of the separation of powers, each branch of government may have a role in calling the other branches to account. So in the UK House of Commons, the system of departmental select committees is meant to make the government (prime minister, cabinet) accountable for its decisions and actions. And we have seen numerous opportunities for accountability to take place in American government. These include:

- investigations of the executive branch conducted by congressional standing or select committees

- the House of Representatives' power to impeach any federal executive or judicial official — including the president — and the Senate's power to try them and, if found guilty, remove them from office
- congressional primary elections, in which incumbent members of the House and the Senate have to fight for the right to appear on the ballot in the general election
- propositions, referendums and recall elections can increase the accountability of state government politicians

Accountability is clearly enhanced by 'knowledge' and 'information'. In a country such as the United States, with a Freedom of Information Act, accountability is likely to be more rigorous than in the UK, with its Official Secrets Act.

B Authority

Authority is **the right to exercise power**. Another key political concept closely allied with authority is therefore **legitimacy**. All political office-holders have a certain degree of authority. In a democracy, where office-holders will often be elected, the election itself bestows a certain authority or legitimacy on the office-holder. People are often described as being 'in authority'; in other words their right to rule can be traced back to the particular office — prime minister, president, senator.

A further matter regarding the concept of authority which is often discussed is 'Where does it come from?' Those on the left in politics — people we would describe as liberals or social democrats — tend to believe that authority 'rises from below', from 'the people'. Those on the right in politics — people we would describe as conservatives — tend to believe that authority 'comes from above' by virtue of political wisdom, social experience or position. (Indeed, if this line of thought were taken one stage further, we would arrive at a belief in 'divine right' — authority bestowed by God.)

It is very important to distinguish 'authority' from 'power'.

C Power

> In answering an essay question including the word 'power', 'powerful' or 'powers', it is always a good idea to spend a few sentences at least making these distinctions clear. Examiners will reward this.

Whereas authority is the right to exercise power, power is the ability to exercise power. But not only must we distinguish 'power' from 'authority', it is very useful in the study of politics to be clear about the distinction between 'power' and 'powers'. **Powers are the functions, tasks or jobs of an office. Power**, on the other hand, **is the ability to get things done**. Every American president has the same powers as his predecessor. Essentially, President Barack Obama has the same *powers* as Jimmy Carter had, as Harry Truman had, as Woodrow Wilson had, as Abraham Lincoln had, as George Washington had — the powers to sign and veto bills, to appoint cabinet officers and Supreme Court justices, to negotiate treaties and so on. But the *power* that each president possesses is very much a variable. Indeed, it even varies for the same president throughout his period of office. One might argue, for example, that Nixon (after Watergate), or Reagan (after Iran–Contra), or Clinton (after Lewinsky), had much less power than before those unfortunate episodes.

Power is the ability to get people to do the things they wouldn't otherwise do. In his scholarly book on the American presidency (*Presidential Power*), Professor Richard Neustadt makes it clear that 'powers are no guarantee of power'. In other words, the jobs one has to do as president are no guarantee of actually getting things done. We saw this in Topic 6.E.1. That is why the president has to resort to **persuasion**. As Neustadt again claims: 'The president's power is the power to persuade.' He does allow that 'powers may lead to power', but they are no guarantee of it.

Checks and balances are all about the **limitation of power**. In this sense, one could make out a good case for the British prime minister being potentially more powerful in terms of pursuing their domestic policy agenda than is the American president.

D Democracy

The quotation comes from Lincoln's Gettysburg address in 1864.

Democracy is, in its simplest definition, **rule by the people**. But that poses other questions: 'What does it mean to rule?' and 'Which people?' President Lincoln's famous remark about 'government of the people, by the people and for the people' is often quoted as an elaboration on our basic definition. The theory of democracy enshrines another important principle — that of **popular participation** in free, fair and frequent elections in which there is political equality for all ('one person, one vote') and freedom of choice between candidates.

So we can begin to judge how 'democratic' a country is by using these criteria. In the USA, we have seen that a large number of national public officials are subject to direct election — the president and vice-president (though still in theory through the Electoral College), senators (since 1914), members of the House. This contrasts quite sharply with the situation in the UK, where no members of the executive branch are directly elected to their executive posts and only members of one of the two legislative chambers — the House of Commons — are directly elected. Indeed, it is worth noting that in the USA the second chamber was reformed almost a century ago to be **directly elected**. Recent reform of the UK's second chamber, however, has been to move from a mix of hereditary and appointed members to a chamber made up only of **appointed** members.

Although the prime minister and most cabinet ministers have been directly elected as MPs.

Like cars, democracy comes in many different models. You do not need to know about all of them at this stage, but it is important that you know about two in particular. In **direct democracy** (sometimes referred to as **participatory democracy**), the people participate directly in making decisions. This was seen in its purest form in the town meeting in ancient Athens. Today it is seen in the use of **referendums** in the UK and in **initiatives** used in the individual states of America, though not at the federal level.

A more common model of democracy nowadays is **representative democracy**. This is best thought of as a form of **indirect democracy**. In this model, the people choose their representatives to make decisions on their behalf. This is the form that exists today in the USA, the UK and several other western European democracies.

Andrew Heywood (*Key Concepts in Politics*, Macmillan, 2000) claims the advantages of democracy are that:
- it defends freedom by constraining power
- it promotes popular participation and citizenship
- it strengthens a sense of community
- it guarantees a high level of political stability

Among the disadvantages, Heywood suggests that:
- it gives power to the 'ignorant and poorly informed masses'
- it amounts to 'tyranny of the 51%' — or even less in some cases
- it easily leads to excessive bureaucracy, too much 'compromise' and sometimes 'gridlock'

See also the section on 'Representation' below.

No political party in a UK general election has won more than 50% of the popular vote since 1945. The 1992, 1996 and 2000 presidential elections in the USA all resulted in the election of a president with less than 50% of the popular vote.

E Representation

This is another very important key concept upon which we have already touched in Section D. But again we need to clarify its meaning quite carefully. What does it mean to call a politician — whether in Parliament or Congress — a 'representative' of the people? What does it mean to say that one of their functions is to 'represent' their constituents?

The word 'representative' is thought to have four distinct meanings.
(1) A representative may act as a **trustee**, using their own mature judgement rather than following the 'popular whim'.
(2) A representative may act as a **delegate**, acting purely on the instructions of others. Hence the term 'delegate' being used by those who attend the American National Party Conventions, having been instructed for whom they should vote (see Topic 2.A.3).
(3) A representative may act upon the basis of a **mandate**. This mandate will have been gained not by the representative themselves, but by the political party under whose banner they stood at the last election. This model of representation is based on the belief that a party, in winning an election, gains a mandate to carry out the policies which it presented at the election.
(4) There is what is called the **resemblance** model of representation. This model would suggest that a legislative chamber should be a **cross-section** or **microcosm** of the nation as a whole. This might be reflected in its make-up, for example in terms of gender, race and geographic region. The extent to which Congress — or the UK Parliament or its regional assemblies — is 'representative' in this sense is a matter of constant debate. It throws up such questions as:
   - Does it matter that in 2009, only 75 of the 435 members of the House of Representatives were women?

- And what about the fact that at the same time there was only one African-American members in the Senate, a group that makes up around 10% of the national population?
- Can only women represent women? Can only Hispanics represent Hispanics?
- Should 'affirmative action' programmes now be instituted to redress such 'unrepresentativeness'?

F Rights

A right is **something to which one is entitled**. The term 'human rights' is therefore used to refer to the entitlements of all humans as humans. (The same could be said, I suppose, of animals and animal rights.) Human rights are often therefore described as being **fundamental** and **inalienable**.

Inalienable = non-transferable, undeniable.

As the American Declaration of Independence has it: 'We hold these truths to be self-evident, that all men are created equal, that they are endowed by their Creator with **certain unalienable rights**, that among these are life, liberty and the pursuit of happiness.'

The term 'rights' is also closely linked with **freedoms**. In the **Bill of Rights**, the Founding Fathers wanted to protect, guarantee and entrench certain fundamental rights and freedoms such as:
- freedom of religion, speech, the press and assembly (1st Amendment)
- the 'right to keep and bear arms' (2nd Amendment)
- the right to remain silent (5th Amendment)
- the right of a 'speedy and public trial' (6th Amendment)

A distinction can be made between negative and positive rights. **Negative rights mark out 'freedoms from'** and **limit** the role of government, for example freedom from 'cruel and unusual punishments' (8th Amendment). **Positive rights mark out 'freedoms to'** and **make demands on** the role of government, for example the right to education.

How and by whom are rights protected? In the USA, we can see that all three branches of government have a role to play: Congress by the passage of appropriate legislation; the executive by proper enforcement of the laws; the courts by interpreting both the laws and the Constitution. Clearly, in a country with a written Constitution embodying a Bill of Rights, the courts have a very important role to play in the protection of rights and freedoms.

G Pluralism

Pluralism is best thought of as **diversity**. Its opposite is **élitism**, best thought of as 'a few'. To describe a country as being pluralist is, therefore, to suggest that the political resources within that country — money, expertise, access to the mass media etc. — are widely spread, and are in the hands of many diverse individuals and groups. This prevents there being a **governing élite**, which would have a **monopoly** of political power.

Pluralism is also associated with **decentralisation**. In the USA, there are so many levels of government that no single group can ever dominate. In a pluralist society, therefore, there is a great need for negotiation, compromising, deals and persuasion.

Pluralism, however, does not necessarily suggest that all these competing groups are equal. They quite clearly are not. Indeed, some see the system as merely one of **competing élites** — political parties, pressure groups, bureaucrats, business people, the media, trade unionists, educators, lawyers and so on. Harking back to what we studied earlier, one could then ask to what extent these 'competing élites' are 'representative' of their own client groups.

The problem with pluralism is that it can easily lead to what many see as the **atomisation** of both politics and society. And this in turn leads to gridlock — the failure of government to be able to do anything at all. Pluralist democracy may be 'nice', but it sure can be frustrating! But then, as Winston Churchill once remarked: 'No one pretends that democracy is perfect or all-wise. Indeed, it has been said that democracy is the worst form of government except for all those other forms that have been tried from time to time.'

A sound point on which to end.

In a speech in the House of Commons on 11 November 1947.

Answers

Topic 1

1 **(a)** One in which all political power rested with the central (national) government; **(b)** one in which virtually all political power rested with the individual states; **(c)** one in which some political power rests with the central (national) government whilst other equally important powers rests with the states.

2 Article I — Congress; Article II — the president; Article III — the Supreme Court.

3 Two-thirds.

4 Three-quarters.

5 A theory of government by which power is divided between three branches of government — the legislature, the executive and the judiciary — each acting both independently and interdependently.

6 Legislature — makes the laws; executive — carries out the laws; judiciary — enforces and interprets the laws.

7 '…separated institutions sharing powers.'

8 A theory of government by which each of the three branches of government exercises checks upon the powers and actions of the others.

9 **(a)** Those powers granted only to the national government; **(b)** those powers granted to both the national and state governments.

10 '…is over.'

11 The war in Iraq; homeland security post-9/11; the expansion of Medicare; the No Child Left Behind Act; the Wall Street and banking collapse.

Topic 2

1 Natural-born US citizen; at least 35 years of age; at least 14 years' residency; has not served two terms as president.

2 **(a)** An election to select a party's candidate for the presidency; **(b)** a series of meetings to select a party's candidate for the presidency.

3 States moving their primary to a date earlier in the year.

4 The time between the previous election and the holding of the first caucuses and primaries in the next election, when would-be candidates try to get themselves noticed, form exploratory committees and begin fundraising.

5 Choose the presidential candidate; choose the vice-presidential candidate; decide the party platform.

6 When the presidential candidate chooses a vice-presidential running-mate who is distinctly different in terms of region, experience, age and maybe gender, race or religion.

7 Promote party unity; enthuse the party faithful; enthuse ordinary voters.

8   John McCain (Republican) and Russell Feingold (Democrat).

9   They began in 1960 and have been used in every election since 1976.

10 **(a)** 538. **(b)** 270. **(c)** Obama 365; McCain 173.

11 Maine and Nebraska.

12 George W. Bush lost the popular vote but won the Electoral College vote.

13 When women tend to support the Democrats and men the Republicans.

14 The Midwest.

15 The economy.

16 When a strong candidate for a party at the top of the ticket helps congressional candidates of the same party to get elected at the same time.

17 When voters cast their ballots for candidates of two (or more) parties for different offices at the same election.

18 When one party controls the White House whilst the other party controls both houses of Congress.

19 The politician who currently holds the seat.

20 **(a)** A process that enables citizens to vote directly to propose laws (and in some states, constitutional amendments), thereby bypassing the state legislature; **(b)** a process by which voters can effectively veto a bill passed by the state legislature; **(c)** a process by which voters in a state can remove an elected official from office before his or her term has expired.

Topic 3

1   Northeast and west coast tend to be liberal; the South tends to be conservative.

2   The shift of southern conservative Democrats to the Republican Party; the end of the Cold War consensus in foreign policy; polarising presidents; the effect of the 'new media'.

3   Every president since 1856 has been either a Democrat or a Republican; in January 2009, 533 of the 535 members of Congress, as well as all 50 state governors were either Democrats or Republicans.

4   The first-past-the-post electoral system; the diversity of the two major parties.

5   Each individual state has its own Democratic and Republican parties.

6   Parties have lost control of presidential candidate selection; parties have been bypassed by 'matching funds'; television and polling bypass the parties' communication function; campaigns are more candidate- and issue-centred.

7   Parties have fought back to regain some control over presidential candidate selection; modernisation of national party structures and network; growth of 'soft money' in the 1980s and 1990s; moves towards nationalising congressional campaigns; increased partisanship in Congress.

8   The programme of reform upon which the Republicans campaigned in the 1994 mid-term elections.

9 Any three of: Constitution Party, Green Party, Libertarian Party, Natural Law Party, Peace and Freedom Party.

10 The electoral system; federal campaign finance laws; state ballot access laws; lack of resources, media coverage and well-known, well-qualified candidates; ideology; the tactics of the two major parties.

Topic 4

1 **(a)** An organised interest group in which members share and actively pursue common views and objectives to influence government. **(b)** Parties seek to win control of government; pressure groups seek to influence the government.

2 Any four of: business/trade; agriculture; unions; professional; single issue; ideological; group rights; public interest.

3 Representation; citizen participation; public education; agenda building; programme monitoring.

4 Material benefits; purposive benefits; solidarity benefits.

5 Electioneering/endorsement; lobbying; publicity; organising grassroots activities.

6 America is a diverse society; the political system has many access points; political parties are weak.

7 Direct contact with members and staff as well as committees; organising letter, phone and e-mail campaigns; publicising members' voting records; endorsements; fundraising and campaigning.

8 Through *amicus curiae* briefings.

9 They are information-givers; policy formulators; sounding boards; enhancers of participation.

10 Any four of: too much money influence; too much for 'special' rather than 'national' interest; elitism; inequalities of power; revolving door syndrome; inappropriate direct action.

Topic 5

1 Bicameral.

2 **(a)** 435. **(b)** Proportional to population. **(c)** 2 years. **(d)** Be at least 25 years of age; a US citizen for at least 7 years; a resident of the state.

3 **(a)** 100. **(b)** Two per state. **(c)** 6-year terms, with one-third re-elected every 2 years. **(d)** Be at least 30 years of age; a US citizen for at least 9 years; a resident of the state.

4 **(a)** Begin consideration of all money bills; impeachment; elect the president if the Electoral College is deadlocked. **(b)** Ratification of treaties; confirmation of appointments; try cases of impeachment; elect the vice-president if the Electoral College is deadlocked.

5 Pass legislation; conduct investigations; initiate constitutional amendments; declare war; confirm a newly appointed vice-president.

6 Any four of: senators represent the entire state; they serve 6-year terms; they are one of 100; they are more likely to chair a committee; they have greater name recognition; they are more likely to be thought of as presidential and vice-presidential candidates; they have exclusive powers.

7 Acts as the presiding officer; interprets and enforces the rules; refers bills to committees; appoints select and conference committee chairs; appoints majority party members of the Rules Committee; influences the flow of legislation through the House.

8 That the chair of a standing committee will be the member of the majority party with the longest continuous service on that committee.

9 To conduct the committee stage of bills; to conduct investigations (Senate only); to begin the confirmation process.

10 It timetables bills for consideration on the House floor; it prioritises bills through the granting of a Rule.

11 They reconcile the differences between the House and Senate versions of a bill.

12 Committee members are regarded as policy specialists; it is as far as most bills get (pigeon-holing); committees have full powers of amendment.

13 Sign the bill into law; leave the bill on his desk; veto the bill (if the congressional session has ended); pocket-veto the bill.

14 By passing the bill again with a two-thirds majority in both houses.

15 Party; constituents; the administration; pressure groups; colleagues and staff; personal beliefs.

16 Because executive branch members are not physically present in the chambers.

Topic 6

1 Propose legislation to Congress; submit annual budget; sign legislation; veto legislation; act as chief executive; nominate executive branch officials; nominate federal judges; act as commander-in-chief; negotiate treaties; pardon felons.

2 An annual address delivered by the president to a joint session of Congress in which he sets out his proposed legislative agenda.

3 **(a)** 64%. **(b)** The third lowest of any president.

4 'The executive power shall be vested in a president of the United States of America.'

5 Bill Clinton (1999).

6 **(a)** 3. **(b)** 15.

7 An advice-giving group selected by the president to aid him in making decisions.

8 Because they cannot be in both Congress and the cabinet, i.e. they have to resign from Congress to serve in the cabinet.

9 **(a)** Any four of: enable him to engender team spirit; look collegial and consultative; give information; gather information; debate policies; present 'big picture' items; check up on legislation going through Congress; see cabinet members he would not otherwise see. **(b)** Any four of: serve as get-to-know-you sessions; a chance to sort out interdepartmental disputes; catch other members before/after the meeting; an opportunity to see the president; gain prestige back at their department.

10 All executive power is vested in the president; there is no collective responsibility; the president is not 'first among equals'; cabinet officers are not his political rivals; presidents often regard cabinet members as disloyal; the president has EXOP.

11 **(a)** '…needs help'. **(b)** The Executive Office of the President (EXOP).

12 Any four of: policy advice; personnel management; crisis management; liaison with federal bureaucracy; liaison with Congress; running the White House; deciding and executing the president's daily schedule; acting as 'lightning conductors' for the president; ensuring orderly decision-making for the president.

13 'Two halves of a bank note, each useless without the other.'

14 '…the power to persuade.'

15 The vice-president; his Office of Legislative Affairs; Cabinet officers; party leaders in Congress.

16 The president's success (expressed as a percentage) in a given year at winning recorded votes in Congress on issues upon which he took a clear position.

17 Congress; the Supreme Court; public opinion; pressure groups; media; federal bureaucracy; federalism.

Topic 7

1 **(a)** The party's presidential candidate. **(b)** Just prior to the party's National Convention.

2 On a joint ticket with the party's presidential candidate.

3 Gerald Ford (1973) and Nelson Rockefeller (1974).

4 Presiding officer of the Senate; casting a vote in the Senate in the case of a tie; counting the Electoral College votes; becoming president on the death, resignation or removal from office of the president; becoming acting president.

5 '…I may be everything.'

6 Richard Nixon (1953–61).

7 Lyndon Johnson (in 1963); Richard Nixon (in 1969); Gerald Ford (in 1974); George H.W. Bush (in 1989).

8 Hubert Humphrey (in 1968); Walter Mondale (in 1984); Al Gore (in 2000).

Topic 8

1 9.

2 **(a)** The president. **(b)** The Senate. **(c)** Life.

3 The Senate Judiciary Committee.

4 **(a)** John Roberts. **(b)** President George W. Bush.

5 **(a)** Conservative philosophy; literal interpretation of the Constitution; tend to be appointed by Republicans; **(b)** liberal philosophy; read things into the Constitution; tend to be appointed by Democrats.

6   Anthony Kennedy.

7   The power of the Supreme Court to declare acts of Congress, or actions of the executive — or acts or actions of state governments — unconstitutional, and thereby null and void.

8   '…what the judges say it is.'

9   The Supreme Court declared unconstitutional a law banning the ownership of handguns in Washington DC. For the first time, the Court stated that the 2nd Amendment right to 'keep and bear arms' is an individual right.

10 The Supreme Court upheld the Partial-Birth Abortion Ban Act — the first time the Court had declared a specific abortion procedure could be banned.

11 Congress; the president; no enforcement powers; no initiation power; public opinion; the Constitution; subsequent decisions of the Court.

Topic 9

1   A programme that entails giving the members of a previously disadvantaged minority group a head start in such areas as higher education and employment.

2   Unfair discrimination against the majority racial group, i.e. whites.

3   Any three of: *Adarand Constructors v. Peña; Gratz v. Bollinger; Grutter v. Bollinger; Parents Involved v Seattle School District; Meredith v. Jefferson County Board of Education.*

4   Leads to greater levels of diversity; rights previous wrongs; opens up areas of education and employment to minorities; creates a more diverse student body in education; the most effective way to deliver equality of opportunity; it works.

5   Leads to reverse discrimination; can lead to minorities being admitted to courses or being given jobs for which they are ill-equipped to cope; can appear condescending to minorities; perpetuates a society based on colour and race; just a quota system under another name; focuses on groups, not individuals.

6   '…good for America'.

7   **(a)** 41; **(b)** 26.

8   Jesse Jackson.

9   Any two of: Eric Holder (African-American); Ken Salazar and Hilda Solis (Hispanic); Steven Chu and Gary Locke (Chinese-Americans); Eric Shinseki (Japanese-American); Ray LaHood (Lebanese-American).

10 **(a)** Thurgood Marshall. **(b)** In 1967 by President Lyndon Johnson.